# Spirited Men,
## Story, Soul, & Substance

## Brian Doyle

Cowley Publications
Cambridge, Massachusetts

Library of Congress Cataloging-in-Publication Data:

Doyle, Brian, 1956 Nov. 6-
    Spirited men : story, soul & substance / Brian Doyle.
        p. cm.
    Includes bibliographical references.
    ISBN 1-56101-258-0 (pbk. : alk. paper)
    1. Men--Biography. 2. Spirituality. 3. Conduct of life. I. Title.
    CT104.D68 2004
    920.71--dc22

                            2004018749

This book was printed in the United States of America on acid-free paper.

Excerpt from "Spring Azures" by Mary Oliver:
From New and Selected Poems by Mary Oliver, Copyright © 1992 by Mary Oliver Reprinted by permission of Beacon Press, Boston.
Excerpts from songs by Paul Kelly published by Warner/Chappell Music, Inc. Copyright © by Paul Kelly and and used by permission.

Cover design: Gary Ragaglia

Cowley Publications
4 Brattle Street
Cambridge, Massachusetts 02138
800-225-1534 · www.cowley.org

For my dad,
James Aloysius Doyle,
the greatest man I ever met.

# CONTENTS

# ACKNOWLEDGMENTS

**M**any of these pieces first appeared in *The American Scholar,* and I am especially grateful to that admirable journal's editors, first Joseph Epstein and then Anne Fadiman and John Bethell, for taking chances on such unusual prose creatures and for deft editorial suggestions. The essays on William Blake, Van Morrison, Plutarch, Jim Kjelgaard, and Paul Kelly all first saw light in the *Scholar,* a great honor (I mean, really, Saul Bellow and Albert Einstein published pieces in *The American Scholar,* nice company there), and the "The Soul of Plutarkos" shared the *Scholar's* Best Essay award in 2000 with "Cut Time," a terrific essay about boxing and character by Carlo Rotella, which I recommend highly.

The essay on Robert Louis Stevenson first appeared in *The Atlantic Monthly,* and to my editors there—Ben Schwarz, Amy Meeker, Cullen Murphy, and the late Michael Kelly—I am grateful.

And proud—Mark Twain published essays in *The Atlantic,* for heaven's sake.

A prayer for Michael Kelly's soul, wrenched from the world in a ditch in Iraq, and for his wife and children, with only his memory to kiss.

The essay on Paul Desmond first appeared in *River Teeth,* a lovely journal of creative nonfiction published in Ashland, Ohio. My thanks and regards to Joe Mackall, the editor. Then it appeared in *New Letters,* a cool lit'ry magazine in Missouri, edited by a fine writer named Robert Stewart.

Hard-workin' essay, that.

The essay on James Aloysius Augustine Joyce was first "published" in different form as a spoken and sung performance for the Ancient Order of Hibernians in Portland, Oregon. To Chuck Duffy and David O'Longaigh of that admirable clan, my thanks, and thanks too to the composer and singer Roger Doyle, who lent his mellifluous baritone to the evening with the songs of John McCormack.

*That* was a fun night absolutely.

Finally my thanks to Michael Wilt, my editor at Cowley, who shepherded and persuaded and midwifed and defended and articulated and tinkered and believed in this slim curious book from my first muttering about it to him to this very moment when you, a Real Live Reader, are holding it in your fist and reading about how cool an editor Michael is.

Hard-workin' editor, that.

*Brian Doyle*

# Where Holy Lives

This book is a collection of resurrections, restorations, recon-
siderations, appreciations, enthusiasms, headlong solos,
laughing prayers, imaginary meetings with most unusual and
most interesting men.

I wanted to bring these men back to public life, in most cases, or
closer to the public eye, in others—to draw them from the shadowy
corners of the room and beam a grinning light on them, to sing their
stories, to see them fresh and new; and to see them too as very often
men of immense spiritual substance, prayerful fury, enormous
grace, wonderful attentiveness to miracle: in other words, devout
men, in the most real and serious and smiling sense. Men very often
concerned in their work and lives with the moral grapple, with the
sinuous crucial puzzle of love, with the wonderfully mysterious
ways that song and story stoke and spark the heart; which is, as you
know and I know, where holy lives.

Why men? Why not women? Or children? Or herons or sea otters
or damselflies or holy oaks?

Because I am a man, and absorbed by the idea that somehow I
might learn how to be a good man, maybe even a great man, before
I shuffle off this mortal coil, and something about each of the men
in these pages teaches me about being a man: William Blake's
relentless eye for the holy, Robert Louis Stevenson's passion and
mercy, Van Morrison's endless journey toward wonder and rapture,
Paul Kelly's enduring empathy for the ragged brokenness of his fellow human beings, Rider Haggard's idea of honor and friendship as
forms of love, Plutarch's insistence that each man has moral greatness within him like a divine seed.

Each of these troubled talented extraordinary artists fascinated
me enough to commit an essay about their lives and works. Maybe
in another book I will commit such misdemeanors about Annie
Dillard and Flannery O'Connor and Rosemary Clooney and Bonnie

Raitt and Willa Cather and the great modern Irish poet Nuala Ní Dhomhnaill who hardly anyone has heard of but whose wild honest lusty poems buckle my knees. That would be yet another way to learn about being a good man, if you consider, as I do, that one very fine way to learn about men is to study women studying men.

I'd guess that half the readers of this book are men interested in the shifting threads of greatness in other men, and the other half are women, even more interested in the rich mystery of the characters of men.

Look: We are all, male and female alike, absorbed by what we might be at our best. We are all chasing after the mysterious nutritious song of the Creator. We are all riveted by art, by how human beings mill their unique and idiosyncratic talents into stories and songs and paintings and dances and sculptures and photographs and plays and films and moments that break your heart, make you howl with laughter, make you sense, for a brief and stunning moment, how brave we are, how foolish, how brief, how holy.

So this is a book of resurrections and resuscitations of eleven men from the vast soup of human beings before and concurrent with you and me. To my mind these are men of eye-popping accomplishment and character who are overlooked, half-forgotten, sentenced to hagiography, or stashed lifeless in the canon rather than seen as very much alive, very much the sorts of people you'd happily sit and talk with over a pint of good ale. If the reader feels a spark of increased affection or respect or fellow-feeling for the subjects here after reading my accounts of them, I will be delighted. I have spent many happy days and nights in their company, chatting gaily with Stevenson over a bottle of Bordeaux, arguing about the nature of character with Plutarkos, talking at length with Jim Kjelgaard about the intricate lives of weasels and mink, watching Mister Blake's flashing eyes as he talks of his visions of Christ, listening to Mister Morrison's roaring holy poetry, listening to Paul Desmond tease gently about the memoir that he may or may not have written, and on and on.

The one profile subject here you would have no occasion whatsoever to know is the late Bob Boehmer of Oregon, but Bob was the most literary and devout man I ever met, and a really wonderful storyteller, and I include him here because he was my dear friend, because I miss him ferociously, and because I'd really resurrect him if I could. I can't do that, so I tell you something of his hilarious and sweet story, as a sort of prayer for his soul, now traveled beyond my ken.

Bob also seems to me a very fine example of the millions of quiet men and women who are great brave fascinating kind-hearted colorful funny hard-working hard-praying tale-tellers, and by sharing some of his long story I want to celebrate and sing so many who live and die and pray generally unremarked by the world.

We are all storytellers, after all—that, and the headlong pursuit of love, which is the holiest thing of all, and the greatest gift, and the most eloquent proof of God, is what makes us human beings, capable of greatness.

CHAPTER ONE

# Van

*Tell me the facts real straight*
*Don't make me older*
"One Irish Rover"

There was a boy named George Ivan Morrison. He was born in summer. He was the only child. His father was quiet and his mother was exuberant. The big river nearby was the Lagan and the little river was the Beechie. He could hear the moans of ships in the big river from his bedroom in the back of the house. When he was a boy he would walk out of the city and into the wooded Castlereagh hills and walk all day long returning at night to meet his friends at the end of the street by the huge electrical towers, the pylons, where they would sing together, all sorts of songs: Ray Charles, Sonny Terry, Muddy Waters, Joyce White, Hank Williams, Leadbelly, the Carter family, Roosevelt Sykes, Johnny Kidd and the Pirates, Cliff Richard, Jerry Lee Lewis, the Shadows, Dixie Darling, Blind Lemon Jefferson, Jimmy Rogers.

*Meet me down by the pylons,* they would say, *by the pylons.*

Every street was the same in his section of the city, long and straight and lined with brick-faced houses each joined to each. There were several churches on his street and he could hear the silver shivering of bells day and night. There were very few trees. There were trees thick along other streets not far away, big oaks along Cyprus Avenue and Raglan Road, and he would walk along those streets and imagine that he was walking through the ancient forests of Ulster when Conchobor was king, or Fergus mac Roich, or when the sons of Uisliu were chanting their songs, songs so sweet that every beast that heard the song gave two-thirds more milk, and any person hearing the song was instantly filled with peace and joy.

When the boy was three years old he experienced rapture while sitting before a gramophone listening to the American gospel singer Mahalia Jackson. When he was eleven years old he experienced rapture suddenly while walking along Cyprus Avenue. His father bought him a guitar and he learned the chords from a songbook of American country songs. He formed a neighborhood band called Midnight Special which featured a boy playing a lead pipe that he had found in the Beechie River and then he formed a neighborhood band called the Sputniks which included a washboard player and a boy who played a broom handle attached to a tea-chest. They played in movie theaters to audiences of other children there for children's movies. Some of the children watching the Sputniks in the movie theater while waiting for the second feature to begin were seven years old, and who knows what they thought of the guitar player, the odd wee boy from Hyndford Street, *shy as a field hare* as one of his teachers said?

He learned to play the saxophone in three weeks and joined the Aces, who were also the Jokers or the Jacks or the Four Jacks or the Thunderbirds depending on where they were playing that day. The Aces carried their instruments with them on the bus to get to the Working Men's Club or the Harriers Hall or the Brickborough Hall or the Hut on Chamberlain Street. Then the wee shy boy played with the Javelins, who were sometimes Deanie Sands and the Javelins when Deanie Sands sang with them, Deanie Sands being a girl named Evelyn who had polio as a child and callipers on her legs and a great voice. Then he played with the Monarchs, during which time he met a singer named Georgie Fame who was managed by the same guy who managed the Temperance Seven, and then he played with the Manhattan Showband, and then with the Golden Eagles, and then with the Gamblers.

When the Gamblers got a regular booking at a sailors' flophouse that had once been a police station they changed their name to Them, after a 1954 horror movie in which giant ants invade California, and Them started playing howling blues and jump jazz, and by now the odd wee boy was seventeen years old and locally famous for a jazzy voice bigger than he was and for sprinting back and forth along the stage, rolling on the floor, dancing on tables, playing the sax while sitting on a bandmate's shoulders, flinging his shirt into the crowd, and dancing with such frenetic abandon while singing that he as often as not split his trousers.

Within three weeks of their first show at the Maritime Hotel in Belfast people were waiting for hours to get in to see Them, and soon They signed a record contract, and then They got famous, and then They left Ireland for England and America, and although pretty soon thereafter, as time in rock music is accounted, Them had pissed away in contractual squabbles, their lead singer with the big jazzy voice kept on going, first headlong away from Hyndford Street and then, much later, desperately back—*take me back,* he would sing with a vast craving in his voice, *by the pylons, by the pylons. . . .*

## All in the Game

Nearly thirty years later the wee shy lad is on stage in a London club called Ronnie Scott's. Been a long road—thirty records made, some three hundred songs composed, a brief marriage and a lovely daughter, Shana, who now sings with him occasionally as she has a big bluesy voice even though she's a wee slip of a thing. He's had many dozens of bands behind him as he strove for the right mix, the right troupe of men and women on instruments who would help him make the music soar into joyous meditation. That's all he wants, all he ever wanted, he has said many times exasperatedly and grouchily to reporters. "But rock and roll is not set up that way," he has also said. "It's set up to do the opposite. It's set up to stimulate. And the music depends on a lot of factors. That's why I don't really like talking about it. It could depend on whether it rained that day or not. It depends on the chemistry of the moment, who you're playing with, whether they're in tune with the song, or the lyrics, the rhythm. It's all kinds of things. It's meant to be a meditative experience."

On the organ tonight, Georgie Fame, who while he was being managed by the guy who managed the Temperance Seven became the leader of the Blue Flames when they hit it big playing ska at the Flamingo Club in London in 1962 when Georgie was nineteen, but then after Georgie's fame peaked with a jazzy hit called "Yeh Yeh" he found himself eventually composing and singing jingles for commercials including one for Esso before Van asked him to play organ and arrange horn charts for his band in 1988, which he has done with pleasure from that day on, even forming a new version of the Blue Flames to be an occasional Van band, as they are tonight, and now Van leans over to him and mutters, loud enough for the rest of the band to hear, *gee em*, which means the key of G major, which means that the Flames might slide into "All in the Game," which, after Van noodles for a moment on his guitar, they do.

The band knows some sixty songs and has a rough idea what might be played tonight, based on which they've been playing recently of those sixty songs, but only Van knows which one is next. "We have a set list," says Guy Barker, the trombone player, "but it only lasts as long as two or three songs. Then he yells at Georgie, who has an extra mike fixed up to communicate with him, and Georgie passes the message along to us. We improvise about sixty percent of the time. We rarely go through a play list. Van is into another aspect of the music."

On the saxophone, Pee Wee Ellis, who used to play with James Brown, the Godfather of Soul, the Sex Machine, and who not only plays a sharp sax but also sings call and response with Van whenever the urge seizes Van to repeat phrases at whim, or sing whatever comes into his head, which urge comes upon him often, sometimes for ten minutes at a time. The band has learned to adjust to this and simply stretch out and repeat bars as long as Van keeps going; usually he will give some sort of a sign when he is closing up shop— often simply a glance or nod of the head, called "the billy" among Irish musicians. "Van's is a style of singing that can still be heard in remote pockets of Connemara and Donegal," says Paddy Moloney of the Chieftains. "At the end of a song he just rattles on. You don't know when he's going to stop, he doesn't know when he's going to stop, depends what's in him at the time." Paddy likes to tell the story of the time he asked Van to give him the billy at the end of a song and when Van finished his scat singing he shouted *Billy! Billy!*

"All in the Game" is about the last song you might imagine a band of jazz and rhythm and blues musicians of this caliber to slide into. Although they are opening the tune in G major, it was composed in 1912, as the wordless "Melody in A major," by Charles Dawes, a Chicago banker who later served as vice president of the United States under Calvin Coolidge. The simple lyrics—avuncular advice from the narrator to a broken-hearted teenage girl as she sits by a phone that refuses to ring—were composed in 1951 by Carl Sigman. The song was then recorded by Sammy Kaye, Carmen Cavallaro, Dinah Shore, and Tommy Edwards. Edwards' first recording of it, in 1957, is straight pop, and slow; his second, in 1958, speeds it up a hair. In 1964 Cliff Richard records the song. In 1970 the Four Tops record the song. In 1979, Van makes his first album for Mercury

Records, *Into the Music.* Record company wants to issue a single. Singles come with two sides. The A side is "Cleaning Windows," a song about a job Van had at sixteen near Hyndford Street with a boy named Sammy Woodburn who climbed the ladder to the top windows because his legs were longer than Van's. The B side, to everyone's astonishment, is "All in the Game," which Van, with his voice alone (the music never goes faster than the relatively sedate beat Edwards gave it in 1958) turns into a bluesy R&B tune. So somehow, somewhere, a melody begun in an American banker's head early in the twentieth century spun into an Irish singer's head later in the twentieth century and spins out again as a piece of Van music. It's been Vanned, and it is continually Vanned; he never plays it the same way twice.

On the guitar Bernie Holland on the piano Neil Drinkwater on the bass Brian Odgers on the drums there in the back Dave Early and on the horns Richie Buckley and Steve Gregory and let's have a hand for Georgie Fame on the organ Georgie Fame.

Having opened in G, the band enters the "head" of the song, or the song proper—stanzas and chorus—demurely backing their leader, who sings gently, affectionately, with his eyes closed, the lyrics that Carl Sigman wrote in 1951, advice to a lovelorn teenage girl: *Once in a while he won't call / But it's all in the game, child.* . . . He might be advising his own daughter. The band behind him drifts easily through various key changes—a map of the song, in fact, looks like a DNA ladder: GCGDBEBCDAADDGCCDGCG-GCGCGCGCGGCGCGCGCGBC, to which Georgie adds a masterly Hammond B3 organ solo (in GCGDGCGDGCGDGCGD), Van finishing the whole thing with a made-up-on-the-spot closing vocal (in GCGCGCGCGBC), the vocal including a spot of wordless scattish moaning in C—and gradually, at Van's subtle direction, speeds up to the point where the song that began in 4/4 time finishes in something closer to 12/8 time, a not-uncommon blues beat, here applied to a song that began as something like a standard 8-bar blues and finished as something like a 16-bar blues without a second chorus and with an extra "tag," or bar's worth of music.

Or, to translate: they jammed through a phrase, played the head once through, played the bridge, quieted while Georgie took a solo (the drummer shifting from the high-hat to the ride cymbal, and going to a "stick click," a gentle crisp sound that keeps the beat while the Hammond moans and growls), then picked it up (Van gesturing to the drummer to hit harder), rising to a crescendo, played an extra bar at that fever pitch at another signal from Van, and finished with a brassy flourish.

But the words here on the page are shadows of what has happened on the stage of Ronnie Scott's club tonight. They're tracks, footprints, marks—a tuft of fur left on a bush in passing, spoor in the snow. They don't catch Georgie's skill and pleasure in fingering an instrument with an infinite number of possible timbres, a machine that began in New York a century ago as a "teleharmonium" designed to send music through electric wires, a machine that Georgie has played for hours every day for four decades. They don't catch the way Georgie plays six quick rhythmic notes as a signal to the drummer to pick up the pace. They don't catch the drummer's instinctive decision to relax to a quiet groove (or "sit in the pocket," as drummers say) a beat *before* Georgie opens his solo. They don't catch the camaraderie of the bassist and the drummer, who like all rhythm sections in all bands of whatever sort drive all ships through all waters. They don't catch the odd way Van plays the guitar with a pick on his thumb, or how he swerves off the lyrics in the second chorus and makes up his own tender advice to the girl waiting lonely by the phone, or how at the end he is again singing with his eyes closed and his head thrown back, singing *I want to lose myself I want to lose myself* as the music washes over him like water and the band builds to a crescendo and then just before the bar ends Van shouts *make it real one more time* and the band plays one more rousing chorus before Van lifts his guitar to signal the flourish and with a howling of horns,

the song ends.

As the packed house begins to roar Van turns away and nods to Georgie who grins and then Van half-bends half-kneels to pick up something from the stage—a glass of porter, it turns out, which he sips from and then places gently on a speaker—but the half-kneeling as he goes for the glass looks like nothing so much as a genuflection.

## Cú

There was a boy named Setanta Sualdaim mac Roich. He was an only child. He was born somewhere west of Belfast and north of the River Boyne. His mother was Deichtine, the sister of Conchobor the king of Ulster, and his father was Sualdam mac Roich, although some say that his father was really Lug mac Ethnenn, a prince of the *dine,* the hidden people.

He was reared in a house of oak on a plain. When he was seven years old a ferocious hound attacked him and he killed the dog. To pay for its death he vowed to protect the owner's herds of sheep and cattle himself and so he earned a new name: Cú Chulainn, the Hound of Chulainn.

There are many stories and songs about the Hound—that he was so fast he could catch a stag in full flight, and catch the shot from his own sling before it hit the earth; that he was so hardy he slept on two great blocks of stone; that he woke so furiously from sleep that no one dared wake him from slumber; that he could go sleepless from the last day of summer until the first day of spring; that he could carry twice his own weight on his back; that he could stand on a spear-point without bloodying his feet; that like a great salmon he could leap twenty times his own height; that he could juggle nine apples with never more than one in his palm; that he could keep a golden apple in the air with his breath alone; and that he could step on a lance in flight and straighten it and then balance atop the point.

His hair was brown at the roots and red in the middle and blonde at the ends. He wore it in three thick coils which fell past his shoulders, and into his hair were tied a hundred red threads. Crimson was his color and so his layered-leather shield and tunic and shirt were deep dark red. He wore a cloak that made him a shadow to his enemies, a concealing cloak made of cloth from Tir Tairngire, the Land of Promise, given to him by his fairy-father Lug mac Ethnenn, who had the magic of the hidden people.

When Cú Chulainn was seventeen years old he held off the armies of Connacht invading Ulster by first harrying them from the hills with his sling, which killed a hundred men, and then by battling them in river-fords, first one by one and then in groups of seven and nine, which battles slew a thousand. Finally his beloved foster-brother Ferdia mac Damain meic Dairi came to fight him at a ford near Fuiliarnn. They fought for three days, each night sending each other food and sweet herbs as medicines for the wounds they had made in each other during the day. They fought so bitterly that the river itself fled its bed in terror to give them room for their warfare.

At the end of the third day Ferdia fell into Cú Chulainn's arms and the Hound dragged him to the north side of the river, so that he would die in Ulster, and there by the river he mourned and lamented for a long time. Cú Chulainn was himself so pierced and wounded by his many battles that not one inch of his body was without evidence of his hard life. Presently he fell into a trance and his healing was so long that he appears but once in all the rest of the Tain Bo Cuailnge, the old stories of the people of the north of Ireland; although there are stories of him later, among them the story of his final battle, and how he held his enemies at bay for three days by tying himself to a stone so that they would see him erect and sword in hand, even as his wounds were such that he filled a lake with his blood, an otter in the lake drinking his blood as his reason and vision began to desert him, and he dreamed dark dreams; but there was a deep spring of stern valor in him, and his unfathomable spirit sustained him, even in his darkest hour, and he remained invincible until his last breath.

Cú Chulainn had two beloved foster-brothers, men he loved and revered, Ferdia mac Damain and Fergus mac Roich, and he had a wife, Emer of the Gardens of Lug, with whom he lived in love until the day of his death, but his best friend was his constant companion Laeg mac Riangabra, who drove his chariot and arranged his weapons. Laeg it was who helped him into his battle-armor, and counseled him, and ministered to his wounds, and encouraged him in war, and mourned with him. And when the deepest sadness was upon Cú Chulainn, and it seemed as if he would allow himself to die of despair on the bloody riverbank by the waters of Fuiliarnn, it was Laeg who listened, Laeg who understood, Laeg whose friendship brought him back from the land of despair to the land of wordless joy.

### *Fame*

Georgie's tour opened in a little English village called Leigh, between the rivers Dee and Ribble, where he was born in 1943 and christened Clive Powell. At age sixteen he was working in a local mill like any sensible Lancashire boy. Then his family went vacationing in Wales, and the keyboard player for a local rock band got sick, and young Clive filled in for him, and he was so good that he was asked to join the band, which he did, but soon after that in the entropic way of rock bands the band disbanded, and Clive in the way of footloose English boys for a thousand years washed downstream to London, where he ended up playing organ in a bar in the East End, where a man named Lionel Bart heard him and suggested he audition for a rock impresario named Larry Parnes, who was impressed with Clive's talent but not his name, and so he signed and rechristened the lad at the same time.

Parnes' biggest star in 1961 was a singer named Billy Fury, who was backed by a band called the Blue Flames, who perhaps had modeled their name and game on James Brown's band, the Famous Flames. The Blue Flames invited the kid from Leigh to join them on the Hammond B3 organ. A few months later Billy Fury fired the Blue Flames, but by then the kid on the organ was the talk of London, and Georgie and the Blue Flames got a regular gig at the Flamingo Club. Their nights at the Flamingo were soon such hot stuff that Georgie and the Blue Flames cut a record—*Live at the Flamingo!*—and started touring to promote it, which tours (one with the rock legend Eddie Cochran, who died suddenly during the tour) brought them to Belfast, where, at about the time that Georgie makes the newspapers for demanding that he and the Flames be given an unheard-of *two whole hours* for their show at a local ballroom, the wee shy boy from Hyndford Street is causing a ruckus four times a night seven nights a week at the Maritime Hotel. At this point Georgie is a grizzled twenty-one years old and Van is all of nineteen.

In November of 1964, the British music magazine *New Musical Express* released its pop charts. At Number One, the most popular song in the United Kingdom, "Yeh Yeh" by Georgie Fame and the Blue Flames. At Number 23 and rising fast, a tune originally written by the American blues singer Big Joe Williams, "Baby Please Don't Go," by the Irish group Them, featuring Van Morrison.

For two more years Georgie and the Blue Flames were perhaps the most popular and renowned band in England, and aspiring musicians—among them drummer Mitch Mitchell, who would later play with Jimi Hendrix—vied to be the next Clive Powell, the teenage sensation immediately invited into the band. But then in 1966 Georgie disbanded the Flames and began a period of twenty years in the musical desert, a time highlighted by occasional rapture (touring Europe with the Count Basie Orchestra) but far more than occasional dreck: television shows, cabaret productions, and uninspired recordings (among them, God help us all, "The Ballad of Bonnie and Clyde"). Finally Georgie was reduced to composing commercial jingles for Esso Oil.

Then one day in 1988 Georgie's phone rang. It was his son, a studio engineer who had just finished working a recording session with Van. Georgie's son, let us say, remarks to his father that he just spoke briefly with Van Morrison, who lit up at the news that Georgie Fame was the engineer's father; and Van, let us say, told stories of catching Georgie and the Flames at the Flamingo, and at the Maritime Hotel in Belfast, and a roaring drunk together once through the East End which finished with two Flames and three Them in the drunk tank and me and Georgie singing like larks at Nelson's pillar which surely set the Admiral spinning in his grave, eh, and how is your da these days, then? He was the greatest man behind the Hammond organ in all the world you know, here's my phone number, have him give me a jingle will you? Georgie Fame, he was a fecking genius. . . .

And later that day, let us say, after drinks and before dinner, Georgie fingers the scrap of paper and figures *ah what the hell* and calls, and a dark suspicious growl answers, and Georgie says yeh, Van, listen, this is Georgie Fame, and the suspicion at the other end drops like a stone and in this manner Georgie and Van renew the sinew of their friendship, laid aside in the days of their youthful abandon, and swore it anew as comrades in arms in the maturity of their years and the fullness of their powers, and fared forth together in pursuit of wordless joy, Georgie restored from jingles for Esso and Van restored to performing live on stage which act he had for seven years with malice abandoned, considering it foul fare for George Ivan mac Morrison born between the Lagan and the Beechie. So by Fame he was reborn to joy.

### Astral Weeks

On September 25, 1967, at 7 p.m., at a studio called Century Sound in the theater district of New York City, a group of jazz musicians gathered. They were session men, hired to play until midnight. On drums, Connie Kay, whose regular group was the Modern Jazz Quartet. On the vibraphone, Warren Smith. On bass, Richard Davis, who had played with Miles Davis. On guitar, Jay Berliner, who had played with Charles Mingus. On flute, John Payne, who had just dropped out of Harvard. The singer, and leader, was the wee shy boy from Hyndford Street, who had just turned twenty-two years old, married an American who called herself Janet Planet, and moved to Boston.

"We were used to playing to charts," remembers Berliner, "but Van just played us the songs on his guitar and then told us to go ahead and play exactly what we felt." Payne remembers that Van "seemed spaced out, he appeared as if he was in a lot of personal pain." There were no rehearsals. When Van finished sketching the four songs he wanted to record that night, the musicians simply began. "These guys just jammed together," remembered another musician there that night, a bassist named John Kielbania, who had played with Van in Boston and came to the session hoping to sit in. "They went right through those songs and then cut all the solos out [in the later editing process, during which harpsichord and strings were added]. If they hadn't done that, every track would have been the whole side of an album." Berliner didn't arrive at the studio until 9 p.m., so the first two songs recorded, "Cyprus Avenue" and "Madame George," featured Van on guitar. Berliner played on the third, "Beside You," and Payne played his flute on the last, "Astral Weeks," which was recorded on its first and only take. "Van never discussed the song," recalled Payne. "He never said anything."

Three weeks later, on October 15, the same musicians gathered again, this time at dusk, and recorded four more songs in the same odd fashion. "There's a certain feel about a seven o'clock session," said Richard Davis, the bassist. "You've just come back from dinner, some guys have had a drink or two, it's this dusky part of the day, and everybody's relaxed. I remember that the ambience of that time of the day was all through everything we played." From this session came "Sweet Thing," "Ballerina," "The Way Young Lovers Do," and "Slim Slo Slider," on which Van, who had learned the sax in order to be admitted to the Aces, finished the song with a sax solo that sounds, as he says, "like it's coming from across a lake."

So, in the space of about ten hours in the crisp early days of one autumn in Manhattan, came *Astral Weeks,* "still the most adventurous record made in the rock medium, and there hasn't really been a record with that amount of daring made since," says Elvis Costello, who was born Declan Patrick MacManus near the river Thames, an only child whose father was a trumpeter, whose mother ran a record shop, and who counts among his foremost musical influences one Georgie Fame.

Even the man who made *Astral Weeks* is not altogether sure what happened. "Originally it was supposed to be an opera," says Van. "By opera I mean multiple visual sketches. I thought I'd do an album that was just singing, and songs that were about something." He can trace some footprints—Cyprus Avenue is the street in Belfast where he experienced rapture under the trees, Madame George was first Madame Joy, named for a clairvoyant aunt in Belfast—but in the end Van is honest enough to say that he cannot explain the music he makes and does not wish to try; a theme he has sounded for nearly four decades in nearly every one of the hundreds of interviews he has been forced to endure. "There's really nothing to talk about when you discuss it," he says. "It's just what I wanted to do at that particular time, so I did it."

## Antithesis

The first time I laid eyes on Van Morrison, or properly on his filmed image, was in a smoky bar in Boston on a night when a movie was being shown on a large white wall in the rear of the bar. This was the first of a short-lived series of free movies shown by the proprietors in an informal setting. Turned out there were several problems with showing a movie on a large white wall in the rear of the bar: the grainy plaster of the wall made it appear that human figures in the movie had skins like lizards, every time a patron stood up his or her shadow entered the movie, and there was a constant parade of shadows passing through the movie because the bathrooms were in the rear of the bar and nature was yelping every two minutes and so were the other patrons when someone moved through the movie on the way to the rear of the bar.

The movie that night was Martin Scorsese's *The Last Waltz*, a documentary of the last public concert, on Thanksgiving Day in 1976, by the original members of the Band, Robbie Robertson Rick Danko Garth Hudson Richard Manuel Levon Helm, with various friends and guests, Joni Mitchell Eric Clapton Bob Dylan Neil Young Doctor John Muddy Waters, and as one guest artist leaves to applause, the Band still rocking along as the next artist prepares to enter stage right, crowd noise in the movie swells, *Ladies and Gentlemen Mister! Van! Morrison!* shouts the master of ceremonies at the Winterland Theater in San Francisco, I lean forward in my sticky seat in the bar in Boston to see what human creature makes the incredible voice that has riveted me already for years . . . and out swaggers a little short stout man in an unfortunate sequined cranberry leisure suit with a lace-up crotch, his double chin crowding the wide wings of his collar, most of his hair past tense, what remains sailing off east and west in wings near as wide as the collar, he is a little round cocky ground squirrel of a man, I stare openmouthed: *Van is a little fat guy!* and then the band smooths out and he opens his mouth and out comes that Voice slicing through the smoke and beery clatter like a shouted rhythm and blues blade.

"We could hardly believe that the short, pudgy replica of the gray nerd who sat behind you through a whole semester of Driver Education and never spoke a word, that absolute antithesis of every Superstar image ever stamped in our skulls, could be the helmsman of this wild night's ride," wrote the rock critic Lester Bangs. I read that remark years later and yelped with delighted surprise, for that had been the exact feeling I'd had in the smoky bar in Boston, sitting there with my jaw hanging open as Van strutted exuberantly off stage after an incendiary version of "Caravan." Van Morrison, a musical genius, the greatest white soul singer ever, creator of music and emotion unlike any musician before or since, *is that guy?*

Yep.

Substance and illusion, that's the lesson. Packaging is a fool, a lie, a dog that don't hunt, a pile of manure, a baloney sandwich, a sneer in the ear, a dodge, a maneuver, a sleight of hand. There's substance on this side of the river and illusion on that side and they are brothers who fight so bitterly that the river where they battle flees its bed in terror as the brothers who love each other hammer each other nigh unto death. Substance wears a concealing cloak that makes him a shadow, a cloak from the land of promise.

## Take Me Back

From July of 1986, when Mercury Records released *No Guru, No Method, No Teacher,* to September of 1991, when Polydor Records released *Hymns to the Silence,* Van Morrison produced six records, each superb—among the greatest sustained bursts of musical creativity in the twentieth century. After *No Guru* came *Poetic Champions Compose* (1987), *Irish Heartbeat* (1988, with the Chieftains), *Avalon Sunset* (1989), *Enlightenment* (1990), and *Hymns to the Silence* (1991). "Why is it," asked Bruce Springsteen in 1990, "that Van Morrison releases a record of genius every year, and no one notices? Why is that?"

*No Guru* opens with a song called "Got to Go Back," about his childhood. *Poetic Champions* has a song called "Give Me My Rapture," about his childhood. *Irish Heartbeat* has a song called "Carrickfergus," about a town just north of Belfast (where Jonathan Swift lived and William of Orange landed). *Avalon Sunset* has a song called "Orangefield," about his grade school. *Enlightenment* has a song called "In the Days Before Rock 'n' Roll," about his childhood. *Hymns to the Silence* has a song called "Take Me Back," in which he sings *Take me way back, when everything made more sense, when you walked down an avenue of trees on a golden summer day, when I understood the light,*

> When you lived, when you lived
> When you lived, in the light
> When you lived in the grace
> In the grace, in grace
> When you lived in the light
> In the light, in the grace
> And the blessing.

Near the end of *Hymns to the Silence* there is a song called "On Hyndford Street." Van doesn't sing this, exactly; he intones it, or chants it, or muses rhythmically aloud, over gentle humming droning music, and it has an eerie hypnotic quality to it, as if he is trying to pray or sing or chant himself back into his bedroom near the Beechie River:

> Take me back, take me way, way, way back
> On Hyndford Street
> Where you could feel the silence at half past eleven
> On long summer nights
> As the wireless played Radio Luxembourg
> And the voices whispered across Beechie River
> And walks up Cherry Valley
> On sunny summer afternoons
> Picking apples from the side of the tracks
> That spilled over from the gardens on Cyprus Avenue
> Watching the moth catcher working the floodlights in
>     the evenings
> And meeting down by the pylons . . .
> Going up the Castlereagh hills
> And the Cregagh glens in summer and coming back
> To Hyndford Street, feeling wondrous and lit up inside
> With a sense of everlasting life . . .
> And voices echoing late at night over Beechie River
> And it's always being now, and it's always being now
> It's always now . . .
> On Hyndford Street where you could feel the silence
> At half past eleven on long summer nights
> As the wireless played Radio Luxembourg

And the voices whispered across Beechie River
And in the quietness we sank into restful slumber in silence
And carried on dreaming in God.

©Van Morrison/Caledonia Productions, Inc.

## *Into the Mythic*

There are a thousand stories about George Ivan Morrison, born in Belfast in 1945 and peripatetic since. He is a legend and stories swirl about him like dark birds. Perhaps he is a legend largely because he does not wish to be. He appears offstage one minute exactly before he is due onstage. He leaves the theater ten minutes after the encore. He is happiest while feeding birds in his garden. He is a sucker for chocolate ice cream. He once told an interviewer that he eats nine full meals a day. He told another interviewer that he has never in forty years performed a song the same way twice. He may or may not be married to Michelle Rocca, who was once Miss Ireland. He always sits with his back against the wall. He will eat a sandwich only if the crusts are neatly deleted. He once found an interview so onerous that he ran off down the street trying to elude the interviewer, who ran after him, and who later wrote bitterly that Van had "the belly of a baker and skin the color of boiled cabbage." To the author of a book about him he sent a letter listing the thirty-six mistakes in it. He and Paddy Moloney of the Chieftains once plotted out a whole album while walking through St. Stephen's Green in Dublin. He has received an honorary doctorate of letters from the University of Ulster. He has received an Order of the British Empire award from the Queen of England. He has expressed interest in teaching philosophy at Belfast University. He is fond of leaving the stage while shouting *Soul! Soul! Soul!* He has said that "sometimes I feel like Phil Spector and sometimes I feel like Howard Hughes." He once stopped in the middle of a concert in Holland and suddenly recited the Lord's Prayer. In recent years when he performs indoors he does so with the theater blazing with light. He once organized and funded a conference at which one of the sessions was entitled "The Effect of Music Upon Hormonal Secretions in the Endocrine Gland." He has sung with Richard Gere and Kermit the Frog, among many other unusual artists. His songs have been performed by Helen Reddy and Richard Hell, among many other unusual artists. His songs have appeared in films directed by Martin Scorsese, Wim Wenders, Francis Ford Coppola, and David Lynch, among others. His song "Gloria" (written when he was nineteen) is perhaps the most-performed song in rock history. He recorded a version of Cú Chulainn's saga for a cassette issued by a company called Moles of Bath. He has for some years now lived on the Salisbury Plain in England between the Severn and Stour rivers, in what was in King Arthur's time called the Vale of Avalon. He has said that his favorite single concert, among the many thousands he has done, was for a handful of people on a winter night in the Church of Saint Stogumber in the Vale of Avalon, a free concert arranged by the local schoolteacher. Michelle Rocca, asked to sum up Van in a line, wrote that he was "honest, mordant, and funny." His favorite television show is *Fawlty Towers*. The Irish poet Paul Durcan has called him the greatest Irish poet since Patrick Kavanagh. A Welsh plasterer from Merthyr Tydfil now makes his living as a Van Morrison impersonator. Van's song "Days Like This" became the unofficial anthem of the Northern Irish peace process in the late 1990s, sung in bars and squares and streets and docks, echoing in Belfast where he had long ago been the wee shy lad from Hyndford Street.

## George, Washington

The greatest river in North America is the Columbia, which begins high in the Canadian Rockies and drains seven American states and two time zones and a vast Canadian province before cramming itself down the throat of the Pacific Ocean. In it are the biggest freshwater fish in the world, sturgeon, which get to be as long and heavy as Cadillacs. On its way through Washington and Oregon the Columbia cuts through a thousand miles and canyon walls a thousand feet high. It roars past farms and ranches and forests and a nuclear reactor that no longer reacts. It is dammed by fourteen dams, one of which is the largest concrete thing in the history of the world, the Grand Coulee Dam, which is a mile across and irrigates a million acres and has a spillway twice as high as Niagara Falls. *Mightiest thing ever built by man,* wrote Woody Guthrie of it in 1941, when he was hired to make songs about how great the dam was. He wrote twenty-six songs in a month and then took off running toward his young death but he left those songs behind him and one is called "Roll On, Columbia," which it does, and then some.

Downriver a ways from the largest concrete thing in the history of the world is a place near the town of George where one wall of the river's gorge falls away into a huge sloping cupped hillside, a massive grass bowl tipped into the river. The bowl is big enough to seat 20,000 people and then some. Across the river from the bowl is a sheer basalt wall that looks and acts like an audio speaker on steroids. Some years ago an enterprising soul built a stage in this natural amphitheater and began booking musical performers of international renown into concerts there during the summer, when the weather in central Washington state, on the high plains east of the Cascades, is clear and dry. So came the wee shy boy from Hyndford Street to George, Washington, on the north bank of the Mighty River of the West, on a summer evening near the end of the century.

There were boats in the big river as night fell, more and more of them as the time for the show approached, people who saw no need to buy tickets when you could sail up and anchor behind the stage, and you could hear the moans of their boat horns in the darkening air, and see the flicker of the fires they lit on the sliver of beach across from the stage. The whole hillside was flickering too—the orange dots of cigarettes and joints, the silver and copper glint of eyeglasses, the yellow poles of flashlights.

An eagle floated past, a second eagle, an arrowhead of cormorants, a lanky heron. The heron circled and circled and circled until eventually the whole hillside noticed it and began to cheer and then it drifted away downriver like a leggy blue plane.

At dusk the crowd began to mutter and rumble as dark figures wandered out from the wings and took their places by their instruments but the microphone at center stage remained unattended in its pool of yellow light. Then a black limousine made its way slowly from a tent a few hundred yards away and a small hunched figure dressed in a black suit with a black hat and black sunglasses jumped out and ran into the yellow pool of light and with a snap of his fingers Van began.

He played old songs and new songs, he played songs from Them and songs by Frank Sinatra, he played an old song of his called "Brown-Eyed Girl" which he had several times sworn never to play again, in fact he had sworn from the stage to kill himself if he ever had to play it again, he played gospel songs, he played "Take Me Back," he played "Why Must I Always Explain?," which he sang with a passion unmatched and the strength of three men. He sang fast and furiously, no more than a few seconds between songs, and many times the songs slid one into another without boundaries, as if they were one long river of song, Van keeping one in the air at all times with his breath alone.

For the whole show he stood planted unmoving in the center of the stage, gripping the mike with his left hand and gesturing sharply to the band with his right, the band shifting gears instantly to his signals—key change, extend the bridge, a fifth bar, double a solo— and behind him Georgie Fame grinned and sang with abandon. When Georgie took an early solo during "All in the Game" Van fell into a trance and stood there silent, but once they were over the bridge of the song and near the crescendo Van held the band there for a long moment, chanting *I want to lose myself I want to lose myself* and then roaring *meet me down by the pylons, by the pylons, by the pylons.* When the song ended the crowd roared for a long time and the sound flew across the dark river and boomed off the wall of the gorge and echoed downriver for miles and miles and miles, maybe all the way to the sea.

CHAPTER TWO

# Billy Blake's Trial

A cold January day, Chichester, England. A "fitfully wet day" along the English coast, according to the Sussex *Weekly Advertiser*. Mid-morning—a melancholy time, too early for lunch, too early for whiskey, breakfast a fond memory.

In the Chichester Guildhall a man named Youatt, a minister, strolls into a courtroom. He is a court recorder, charged with short-hand accounting of trial proceedings. The room in which he found himself was probably made almost entirely of wood: wooden benches, wooden railings, a wooden witness-box adjacent to the wooden magistrate's seat, wooden floor, sometimes a wooden judge. There were probably two oil paintings to either side of the magistrate's seat. One was almost certainly of the King—George III at the time. The other was usually of a national hero of some sort; let us say it is a portrait of the genius poet John Milton, a man who looked like a cart-horse. Both paintings were probably enormous, as huge paintings were then considered dashing. No other ornaments are visible in the room, although there were almost certainly mountains of loose papers on the two counselors' tables.

Nothing happens to the Reverend Mister Youatt in his wooden room for a good long while. In a sense this stultifying pause is very English. Nothing happens for long stretches in England. It is the English way—white bread, thin tea, sex on Saturday. A land of hedgerows and gardens, amid which the people dream of order and porter. A slow land, a dreamy land. On this day, however, in about fifteen minutes, Mr. William Blake, age forty-seven, a resident of nearby Felpham for three years, will be tried for sedition against George III, King of England, said treasonous acts being assault and battery on the person of Private John Scolfield of the Royal Dragoon Guards, and dragging the Private down the street by his collar, and stuffing the Private bodily into his barracks, and the vehement utterance of many seditious expressions, viz.: "Damn the King,"

"You Soldiers are all Slaves," and "If Bonaparte should come he would be master of Europe in an Hour's Time," etc., etc. The case, Rex. v. Blake, will be tried before a jury, six magistrates, and the Duke of Richmond. Counsel for the defense, Mr. Samuel Rose. First witness for the prosecution, Private John Cock of the Royal Dragoon Guards. Witnesses for the defense, various.

> Now is my grief at worst, incapable of being
> Surpassed; but every moment it accumulates more & more,
> It continues accumulating to eternity; the joys of God
>     advance,
> But my griefs advance also, for ever & ever without end.
> O that I could cease to be! Despair! I am Despair,
> Created to be the great example of horror & agony; also my
> Prayer is vain. I called for compassion; compassion mock'd;
> Mercy & pity threw the grave stone over me, & with lead
> And iron bound it over me for ever.

Blake was nervous about the trial, damned nervous. It had already cost him a hundred pounds simply for bail—money he had to borrow from friends—and the prospect of losing the case was terrifying. England had declared war on Napoleon in May, the country was an unruly bundle of nerves, and rumors of French invasion were rife along the southern coast. It was also rumored that Napoleon had assembled fleets of flatboats in every creek and harbor on the Channel; to fend off these invaders, troops of dragoons had been quartered in various coastal towns. Thus came Scolfield's troop to Felpham. Under these circumstances few accusations could be more serious than that of sedition, and the fact that Scolfield was a soldier boded ill.

Adding to the actual physical danger of Blake's position was its inconvenient timing. Blake and his wife, Catherine, had spent this last year in Felpham itching to leave. They were ready to move back to London in September when Scolfield filed charges in August. Felpham, which Blake had hoped would be "a sweet place for Study," had been a bust: Catherine was constantly sick, his neighbor William Hayley badgered him incessantly, and the weather was unrelentingly, angrily, eternally grey. London, which he had fled cursing its filth and meanness, now looked delicious. "I can carry on my visionary studies in London unannoy'd," he wrote to his London friend Thomas Butts. "There I can converse with my friends in Eternity, See

Visions, Dream Dreams & prophecy & speak Parables unobserv'd & at liberty from the Doubts of other Mortals. I assure you that, if I could have return'd to London a Month after my arrival here, I should have done so, but I was commanded by my Spiritual friends to bear all, to be silent, & to go through all without murmuring."

What is the price of Experience? do men buy it for a song?
Or wisdom for a dance in the street? No, it is bought with
    the price
Of all that a man hath, his house, his wife, his children.
Wisdom is sold in the desolate market where none come
    to buy,
And in the wither'd field where the farmer plows for bread
    in vain.

In Felpham, Blake had hired a man named William to tend to his garden. The man was an ostler, or horse groom, at the nearby Fox Inn. On the morning of August 12, Blake emerged from his cottage to find two men in his garden. One was William; the other was Private Scolfield, who, unbeknownst to Blake, had been invited into the garden by the gardener.

"I desired [Scolfield], as politely as was possible, to go out of the Garden," Blake explained in a letter to Butts. "He made me an impertinent answer. I insisted on his leaving the garden; he refused. I still persisted in desiring his departure; he then threaten'd to knock out my Eyes, with many abominable imprecations & with some contempt for my Person; it affronted my foolish pride. I therefore took him by the Elbows & pushed him before me until I had got him out; there I had intended to have left him, but he, turning about, put himself into a Posture of Defiance, threatening & swearing at me. I, perhaps foolishly & perhaps not, stepped out at the Gate, &, putting aside his blows, took him again by the Elbows, &, keeping his back to me, pushed him forward down the road about fifty yards—he all the while endeavouring to turn round & strike me, & raging & cursing, which drew out several neighbours; at length, when I had got him to where he was Quarter'd, which was very quickly done, we were met at the Gate by the Master of The Fox Inn (who is the proprietor of my Cottage), & his wife & Daughter & the Man's Comrade & several other people. My Landlord compell'd the Soldiers to go indoors, after many abusive threats against me & my wife from the two soldiers; but not one word of threat on account of Sedition was utter'd at that time."

And then the Knave begins to snarl,
And the Hypocrite to howl;
And all his good Friends shew their private ends,
And the Eagle is known from the Owl.

Three days later Private Scolfield swore out a formal complaint of sedition by the "Miniature Painter" William Blake against the King. Scolfield's account had Blake delivering a lengthy and blood-thirsty speech during which he shouted that he would cut the throats of his fellow Englishmen at Bonaparte's command, among other savageries. Scolfield also swore that Mrs. Blake issued forth from the cottage like a Fury and shouted that "altho' she was but a Woman, she would fight for Bonaparte as long as she had a drop of blood in her." Scolfield's account ends with Mrs. Blake telling her "said Husband" to eject the soldier, with Blake seizing the peaceful Scolfield by the collar, and with Blake damning the King as loudly at the top of his voice.

Cold snows drifted around him:
Ice cover'd his loins around.

The matter went to a grand jury in October 1803 at the Michaelmas Quarter Sessions in nearby Petworth. Blake attended, accompanied by his gardener. To Blake's dismay, the jury found Scolfield's charges of sedition and assault worthy of trial—the "bills were true," in the phrase of the day—which meant that he would be formally tried before a judge and jury in January. It was Blake's right, as defendant, to provide the court with his account of the matter, if he so chose, and to list points of evidence that he or his lawyer would muster in his defense. Blake did so, in a businesslike memo-randum titled In Refutation of the Information and Complaint of John Scolfield, a private Soldier, Etc. The memo ends with this edi-torial flourish:

"If such Perjury as this can take effect, any Villain in [the] future may come and drag me and my Wife out of our House, and beat us in the Garden or use us as he please or is able, and afterwards go and swear our Lives away. Is it not in the Power of any Thief who enters a Man's Dwelling and robs him, or misuses his Wife or Children, to go and swear as this Man has sworn?"

> Los seized his Hammer & Tongs;
>     he laboured at his resolute Anvil
> Among indefinite Druid rocks & snows of doubt &
>     reasoning.
> Enraged & stifled without & within,
>     in terror & woe, he threw his
> Right Arm to the north, his left Arm to the south, & his Feet
> Stamped the nether Abyss in trembling & howling & dismay.

Enter, with a hacking cough, Mr. Samuel Rose. He is a thin and sickly man about thirty years old, a friend of both Hayley and of the poet William Cowper. Hayley, who has already shelled out most of Blake's bail, hires Rose to defend Blake at Chichester Sessions.

The prosecution argued first, as is the custom to this day in English (and American) law, and after statement of the charge by Private Scolfield and corroborating testimony by Private Cock, Scolfield's lawyer hammered away at the "atrocity & malignity" of the charge, figuring that if the jury could be awed by the seditious imprecations that had supposedly issued from Blake's mouth, they would ignore the fact that the only eyewitness, the ostler, was prepared to swear that Blake said nothing of the kind. This tactic, called prosecuting the crime, sometimes works with serious charges, since juries are anxious to assign blame for such crimes; the more serious the offense, the more likely they are to convict someone.

Counselor Rose tooled his defense accordingly. His speech, "taken in short Hand by the Revd. Mr. Youatt," opens with a complete agreement that such an offense is atrocious and malignant beyond words: "If there be a man who can be found guilty of such a transgression, he must apply to some other person to defend him," says Rose, icily. "I certainly think that such an offence is incapable of extenuation. My task is to shew that my client is not guilty of the words imputed to him; it is not to shew that [those words] are capable of any mitigated sense."

Having distanced himself and his client from the devilry of the charge, Rose methodically sets out the pieces of his argument like chessmen. One, Blake has been a loyal subject of the King all his forty-seven years. Two, Blake is a friend of local hero and noted patriot Hayley, who would never have allowed a rebel into his house.

Three, Blake is an artist, and therefore apolitical. ("His art has a tendency, like all the other fine arts, to soften every asperity of feeling & of character, & to secure the bosom from the influence of those tumultuous & discordant passions, which destroy the happiness of mankind.") Four, Scolfield is an undependable witness—he has been broken from sergeant to private on account of drunkenness. Five, the charge prima facie doesn't make sense—is Blake, a sensitive artist, likely to storm from his house to utter "malignant and unintelligible discourse to those who are most likely to injure him for it"? Six, the ostler, who saw and heard the whole row, denies the charge wholly. Seven, the testimony of Private Cock, who stated that he emerged from his barracks to hear Blake damning King, country, and soldiers, is contradicted by a woman named Mrs. Grinder, who was next to Cock by the door of the barracks, and who says the poet said nothing of the kind.

"I will call my witnesses [the ostler and Mrs. Grinder] & you shall hear their account," sums up Rose. "You will then agree with me that they totally overthrow the testimony of these Soldiers. . . ."

At this point, shockingly, Rose collapsed, overcome with the tension and with the effects of a nervous disease that would kill him a few months later. The court was in an uproar for several minutes.

> Lightnings of discontent broke on all sides round
> And murmurs of thunder rolling heavy long & loud
>     over the mountains

Rose was helped to his feet but could not carry on, and because there was suddenly no defense lawyer, the defense witnesses were not called. The chairman of the Bench of Magistrates, the Duke of Richmond (who, according to Hayley, disliked Blake intensely and was for political reasons itching to convict him), sent the jury off to its deliberations, and the packed house settled back to wait for a verdict.

It could not have been much later than two o'clock p.m. when the jury retired; the trial had begun at ten a.m., only the two soldiers had testified, and there had been only one full-length summation, the prosecution's. If we generously allow half an hour for Rose's suddenly aborted speech (it is 1,650 words in Youatt's account), and guess that there was a lunch break, or an adjournment of some kind, or that Blake's repeated shouting of "False!" during Scolfield's testimony (a boy at the trial later told the journalist Alexander Gilchrist that what he remembered best from that day was Blake's "flashing eye") held up matters, or that attending to the fallen Rose may have taken a while, we may have pushed the clock to three o'clock or so. But the jury did not return its verdict until nearly eight o'clock p.m.

So Blake sat there in the courtroom at the Guildhall, on a dank day, his lawyer silenced, his wife sick at home, his freedom and future in the hands of people he did not know, in a county he had been itching to leave for years, for five hours.

How long will ye vex my soul,
And break me in pieces with words?

If this essay was a movie there would be a natural break at this point; the camera would pan around Blake sitting there at the table, his eyes flashing, the murmuring crowd staring at him, the Duke of Richmond glaring from the bench, Scolfield glaring from the prosecution's table, Rose wheezing in a corner, Hayley up in the balcony signing autographs, the Reverend Mr. Youatt leaning back in his chair, exhausted. Perhaps the camera would zoom in on Blake's round face ("he had a broad pale face and a large full eye," wrote the memoirist Crabb Robinson), always keying on his eyes, using the ferocious glare in them as an anchor for the frame. His eyes were gray and slightly protuberant, an effect heightened by his receding hairline. He had a firm chin, a considerable nose, and the look of a furious hawk when he was angry. The camera sidles up to Blake's face, the hubbub in the room gets a little louder, Blake turns slightly to stare right into the camera, his glaring eye FILLING THE FRAME....

Which does a fade-and-flip so fast it barely registers on the viewer, and now the camera is retreating from the same ferocious eye but the eye is in the face of four-year-old Billy Blake, second son of James Blake, hosier and haberdasher, and we are into the flashback scene, which will cover, in a series of cross-cut jumps, the forty-three years between 1761, when Blake, age four, saw God, "who put His head in the window and set him a-screaming," according to his wife, and 1804, when Blake is the quiet eye of a swirling hubbub in Chichester's Guildhall.

And then I think of Blake, in the dirt and sweat of London—
   a boy
staring through the window, when God came

fluttering up.
Of course, he screamed,
seeing the bobbin of God's blue body
leaning on the sill,
and the thousand-faceted eyes.

*Mary Oliver, "Spring Azures"*

At age eight Blake reported to his mother that he had seen the prophet Ezekiel under a tree. His mother beat him. At age ten he reported that he had seen a tree filled with angels, their "bright angelic wings bespangling every bough like stars." His father beat him. A month later, as he stood at the edge of a field watching hay-makers at work, he saw angels walking toward him through the rye. His parents stopped beating him and sent him to art school, a decision made easier by the fact that the boy was a "booby" who spent all his time in his father's haberdashery drawing on the backs of bills. At age fourteen he became an engraver; at age twenty-four he married a slim dark-eyed girl named Catherine, who calmed him by cupping his feet in her hands when he shook with visions.

For the next twenty-three years Blake drew, painted, engraved, printed, colored, stippled, and lithographed. He opened a print shop which immediately went bust. He invented a new form of engraving after he had a dream in which his dead brother Robert explained it to him. He wrote songs and then simple poems and then vast books of complex poems, many of which he engraved and printed himself, in books that he and Catherine painted and bound by hand. They lived on Green Street, Broad Street, Poland Street, the Hercules Buildings, Felpham, South Molton Street, and in the Strand. He sometimes made money and sometimes did not. Mostly he did not. To earn a living he did engravings on commission and drawings and watercolors for books and magazines; meanwhile, at night, at dawn, and often when he was supposed to be working on commissions, he wrote his huge poems and engraved them onto copper plates and printed them and watercolored the sheets and bound them into books, which he offered for sale at outrageous prices.

Here are the names of some of his books: *The Marriage of Heaven and Hell, The Book of Los, The Everlasting Gospel, The Book of Thel, The Book of Urizen, The Song of Los, The Four Zoas, Songs of Innocence and of Experience shewing the Two Contrary States of the Human Soul, Milton,* and *Jerusalem*. These last two were among his last, and both were begun at Felpham, before the trial. It is quite possible that Blake was writing Milton on the morning of August 12, when he walked out into his garden and noticed Private John Scolfield, of His Majesty's Royal Dragoons, standing at the garden gate, with a sneer upon his face.

> If you account it Wisdom when you are angry to be
> silent and
> Not to shew it, I do not account that Wisdom, but Folly.
> Every Man's Wisdom is peculiar to his own Individuality.

Between three o'clock, when the jury retired, and eight o'clock, when the foreman stood to announce the verdict, Blake probably remained seated. Possibly he read, drew, or painted. He apparently had an astonishing capacity for concentration, and many times he spent eight hours at a time writing or drawing. It may be in this case that he simply sat there in the room thinking. There were no rules then, as there are none now, about activity during intermissions in trials; while the jury is deliberating, the accused, if he or she is not physically restrained, may stand on his head, imitate a cricket, mutter poems, or stare abstractedly into space. But this interregnum ends at the moment that the jury files back into the courtroom and the foreman stands and William Blake stands and stretches himself to his full height (about 5 feet 5 inches), and waits to hear whether he is a free man or whether he will be deported to Australia or hung by the neck until he is dead.

> Every Night and every Morn
> Some to Misery are Born.
> Every Morn and every Night
> Some are Born to sweet delight.
> Some are Born to sweet delight,
> Some are Born to Endless Night.

The courtroom hushes; Blake's eyes are nearly popping out of his head as the foreman forms the words
*Not*
and then with a rush as the crowd begins to roar
*Guilty,*
and the courtroom explodes.

"In defiance of all decency," the Sussex *Weekly Advertiser* reported, the court was "thrown into an uproar by noisy exultations," and Blake was rushed out of the Guildhall in a roaring tide of townspeople. Hayley, ecstatic at the verdict, paused to drip some sarcasm on the judge, who he thought "bitterly prejudiced" against Blake: "I congratulate your Grace," said Hayley unctuously, "that after having been wearied by the condemnation of sorry Vagrants, you have at last had the gratification of seeing an honest man honorably delivered from an infamous persecution. Mr. Blake is a pacific, industrious, & deserving artist."

"I Know nothing of Him," snapped the Duke.

"True, my Lord, your Grace can know Nothing of Him," said Hayley, driving home the lance; "& I have therefore given you this Information: I wish your Grace a good Night." And off he went with Blake to dinner at the home of a mutual friend, Mrs. Poole.

I think about that dinner once in a while—what they ate, what Blake thought, who got drunk. Probably Hayley pontificated, as he did that well, and he had, after all, paid Blake's legal fees. I suppose Mrs. Poole smiled happily on her friend Blake, released from the shadow of the noose. And Billy Blake, Billy Blake—did he drink too much? Was he merry? Or did he sit there like a rock in a stream and think about his darling Kate, sick in bed in their new flat in London, and in his mind take her in his arms and tell her Kate, we are free, free, free, Kate, free, and the world will never again bind us and we will forge ahead and make our art and start over and earn our bread and worship the Lord and be free free free free free?

> A Robin Red breast in a Cage
> Puts all Heaven in a Rage.
> A dove house fill'd with doves & Pigeons
> Shudders Hell through all its regions.

William Blake, poet and printer, disappears almost completely from the public record after his trial. From 1804 through 1809 he scrambled without much success to make a decent living as an engraver. In 1809 he held a one-man show of his paintings at his brother's house. The show failed miserably, and its only reviewer, Robert Hunt of *The Examiner* magazine, called Blake "an unfortunate lunatic." In 1812 he exhibited four paintings at the Water Colour Society. In 1816 he was listed in *A Biographical Dictionary of the Living Authours of Great Britain and Ireland,* although the entry made him out to be an eccentric. From 1808 to 1819, Blake sold perhaps a couple of dozen engravings per year. He told an art dealer that he and Catherine made do for many years on an income of about a guinea a week; the equivalent, today, of a couple living for seven days on about twenty dollars. He kept working, though—"I never Stop," he told one friend—and the years slipped by until it was 1827 and he was suddenly seventy years old, "being only bones & sinews, All strings & bobbins like a Weaver's Loom."

> Trembling I sit day and night, my friends are
>     astonished at me,
> Yet they forgive my wanderings. I rest not
>     from my great task!

I have been writing this essay for more than a year now. I have been taking notes for it for five years. Over the course of those years I have asked myself, many times, why I'm doing this. A careful account of the trial for sedition of the poet and printer William Blake, in the year 1804, on a fitfully wet day in January, in a wooden room by the sea—why?

Answering this question is like trying to answer the very good question, Why do you write? I don't know why I write, exactly. Catharsis, the itch to make something shapely and permanent, the attempt to stare God in the eye, the attempt to connect deeply to other men and women, because I can't help myself, because there is something elevating in art, because I feel myself at my best when I am writing well. Because because because. Because this essay is my way of befriending and comprehending Billy Blake, whom I greatly admire in absentia.

Why do you admire him so?

Because he told the truth, because he shoved an insolent leering soldier down the road and stuffed him through a doorway, because he saw angels and saints and talked openly about his visions. Because he published his work himself. Because he was a tender and difficult and solicitous friend. Because he took great pride in his engraving and worked endlessly on plates to make them perfect. Because when he knew he was going to die he lay in his bed singing softly. Because he smiled at the deft poetry of the message when his wife served him an empty plate at dinner to remind him that they were starving. Because he wasn't satisfied with extant mythology and so built a vast grand impenetrable one of his own. Because in all the things he wrote he never mentioned his weight, which was ample, or his height, which was not. Because he single-handedly rescued the ampersand from oblivion. Because in the few drawings of him he is alert, intent, attentive. Because even though he claimed much of his work was dictated whole to him by angels and prophets, he edited heavily. Because he and his wife used to sit naked in their garden and recite passages from *Paradise Lost*. Because when he was asked to recite his poems at parties he got up and removed his coat and sang his lyrics aloud while dancing around the room, which is why he was subsequently not invited to parties anymore. Because he taught his wife, a farmer's daughter, to read. Because he rose first every morning and laid the fire and made tea for her. Because he was endlessly exuberant. Because once at a dinner party he suddenly said to the child next to him, "May God make this world as beautiful to you as it has been to me," a sentence she remembered the rest of her life. Because he held his opinions firmly. Because his wife said she never saw his hands still unless he was asleep. Because to walk with him "was like walking on air and talking with the Prophet Isaiah," said his young friend George Richmond. Because he took great care to leave no debt at his death. Because he wrote and then threw away "six or seven epic poems as long as Homer, and twenty tragedies as long as Macbeth," judging them not worthy of publication or engraving. Because in the ringing fury of his lines there is also great mercy. Because even when he was sick unto death he engraved a little business card for his old friend George Cumberland. Because he could not stop painting and died with his pencil in his hand. Because he bought a new pencil two days before he died. Because the very last thing he drew was his wife's face.

It is this last detail that catches my heart.

> But thou O Lord
> Do with me as thou wilt!
> for I am nothing,
> and vanity.

I have scoured many books for accounts of Blake's last day. I'm not sure why. We all die, in the end, and the grace or gracelessness with which we leave is meat only for the morbid. Yet I want to know how Billy stepped into the next room. I want to know how firmly he held his opinions in the face of annihilation. I want to hear his heart. I want to know him, in the last moments that he wore a body like mine, in the last moments that he saw crows, spoons, apples, angels.

He died on a Sunday in late summer. By this time he was completely bedridden, "his ankles frightfully swelled, his chest disordered, old age striding on," noted a friend. Blake himself knew that he had not long to live. "Dear Cumberland," he had scribbled in April, "I have been very near the Gates of Death & have returned very weak & an Old Man feeble & tottering, but not in Spirit & Life, not in The Real Man, The Imagination, which Liveth for Ever. In that I am stronger & stronger as this Foolish Body decays. . . ."

On the morning of August 12—exactly twenty-three years, to the day, after he met Private John Scolfield, of His Majesty's Royal Dragoons—Blake awoke early and painted for a couple of hours. Then, according to his wife, he said "I have done all I can," and dropped the painting on the floor. She sat down at his bedside.

"Kate, stay as you are. You have been an angel to me, I will draw you," he said. When the drawing was finished he signed it "Mrs. Blake drawn by Blake," and wrote her name in large letters under his signature.

Then he began to sing.

He sang "Hallelujahs & songs of joy & triumph, with true exstatic energy," for the rest of the afternoon—hymns and then, for hours, his own poems. At about six o'clock, he told Catherine that he was going to that country that all his life he had wished to see, and that he would always be about her.

"Then," wrote his friend Richmond (no relation to the Duke), who was at his bedside, "his Countenance became fair, His eyes Brighten'd, and He burst out Singing of the things he saw in Heaven," and he died.

Have pity upon me, have pity upon me,
O ye my friends;
For the hand of God hath touched me.

After a minute Richmond reached over and closed his eyes—"to keep the visions in." Richmond then left. As he paused in the door, he looked back. The last thing he saw, he wrote later, was Catherine kissing William's hands.

Catherine died four years later. She often talked to her husband as if he was in the room, and in her last hours she called continually to him, to say she was coming soon, and would not be long from his side.

It is said that she died with one of his pencils in her hand.

CHAPTER THREE

# The Soul of Plutarkos

As with most of the greatest writers in Western history—
Homer, Shakespeare, the gaggle of anonymous geniuses who
wrote the Bible—we don't know much about Plutarch of
Greece in the usual biographically fussy way. Born in the year 45 or
so, died in the year 120, nearly eighty years old, an unimaginably
long life at a time when living to fifty was a triumph. Student in
Athens when the Emperor Nero visited there in the year 66; traveler
to Egypt and Africa; visitor for a long period in Rome, apparently on
civic business, although he also gave a number of popular lectures
as a sort of visiting professor of history and ethics. Back home to
Greece and his little native village—Chaeronea, in Boetia—which he
was famously loath "to make less by the withdrawal of even one
inhabitant," for the rest of his many years, during which time he
wrote perhaps fifty books while serving as mayor, priest, and inspector of public works—he remarks that his neighbors tease him for
"standing by and watching while tiles are measured out and stone
and mortar brought up." There is no firm record of his death, no
famous funeral oration by a friend, no deathless stone known under
which we might find his dignified bones; but if ever a man was
surely buried where he was born, it was Plutarch, and Greece's soil
is richer for his final return to it.

Thus the skeleton of his life. But let us enflesh him, bring back
some-thing of the personality and character of the man, in the way
he saved so many notable men of his time—alas, few women, mostly
warrior queens—from dessicated hagiography.

His wife was Timoxena, and we know of at least six children
granted Timoxena and her curious husband. The oldest son died; a
second son, "our beautiful Charon," died; Autobulus, Plutarch Jr.,
and Lamprias lived to manhood; and little Timoxena, "born to your
wishes after four sons," as Plutarch Sr. wrote to his wife, "and afford-
ing me the opportunity of recording your name, and a special object

of affection," died while yet a child and while her father was travel-ing. His wife sent messengers, and Plutarch was confronted with the awful news as he arrived in the town of Tanagra.

Imagine our man at this juncture, dusty and tired, an old man by the gauge of his day—he is a grandfather by this time—standing at the gates of the city. He has lived long and hard, studied under the great Egyptian philosopher Ammonius in Athens, traveled to the great capitals of the known world, studied and worked at Rome, the heart of the empire, where he befriended the best and brightest men of his day. Now, retired from imperial fame and happily become a local lion, he's on the road, perhaps on a lecture tour to scrape up some appearance fees, or to Athens on civic business, perhaps to haggle over taxes or tiles. And as he walks in the gate a man rushes up to him and tells him, *Plutarch, news from Chaeronea, your little daughter Timoxena is dead.*

A taut moment there at the gate, the day sliding into evening, the messenger silent, waiting; and Plutarch's body sagging, dust in his throat, a sudden sharp pain in his belly. After a minute he clears his throat and thanks the messenger, hands him a coin. The man walks off, turning twice to look with rising pity on the famous Plutarkos, now bereft of his last child and only daughter, the daughter he held alive in his heart only moments before, thinking of her as he walked down into Tanagra, imagining her finishing her lessons that after-noon in Chaeronea and rushing off to the beach for a swim before dinner and dark.

"Plutarch to his wife, greeting," begins the letter Plutarch wrote from Tanagra, possibly that night. "The messengers you sent to announce our child's death, apparently missed the road to Athens. I was told about my daughter on reaching Tanagra. . . ." He discusses the funeral, and his conviction of their mutual desire that arrange-ments be made "apart from all excess and superstition, which no one would like less than yourself. Only, my wife, let me hope, that you will maintain both me and yourself within the reasonable limits of grief. What our loss really amounts to, I know and estimate for myself. But should I find your distress excessive, my trouble on your account will be greater than on that of our loss. I am not a stock or stone, as you, my partner in the care of our numerous children, every one of whom we have brought up ourselves at home, can testify."

The good character and sweet ways of their late daughter make their loss especially painful, he continues, "yet why should we forget the reasonings we have often addressed to others, and regard our present pain as obliterating and effacing our former joys?" And after recalling with admiration the "perfect order and tranquility" of their home immediately after the deaths of their older boys, Plutarch concludes by repeating his conviction that the human soul is immortal, and that we are sustained in loss by the ancient nurturing rivers of clan and religion.

A most curious and revealing letter, this. Let us imagine Plutarch scratching it out, the scritch of his pen and the quiet snapping of an evening fire the only sounds in the room; below him, in the street in the gathering dark, the small sounds of a town closing down for the night. Plutarch has bathed and eaten lightly after his long journey, but refrained from proffered wine, mindful of the solemnity of the moment and the hole in his heart; and now he sits sadly by the fire, collects pen and paper, and . . . writes at length about the necessity of a tranquil funeral and the avoidance of excessive lamentation? What kind of cold fish is this?

* * *

This kind of fish: Character was everything to Plutarch, both in his own life—in which he aspired to unrelenting service, and rose as high as governor of all Greece and honorary consul of the Roman Empire (according to the historians Suidas and Syncellus) and priest of Apollo at Delphi—and in his literary work, all of which was made, as he said, to explore the souls of his subjects. "My design is not to write histories, but lives," he begins his account of Alexander the Great. "And the most glorious exploits do not always furnish us with the clearest discoveries of virtue or vice in men; sometimes a matter of less moment, an expression or a jest, informs us better of their characters and inclinations, than the most famous sieges, the greatest armaments, or the bloodiest battles whatsoever. Therefore as portrait-painters are more exact in the lines and features of the face, in which the character is seen, than in the other parts of the body, so I must be allowed to give my more particular attention to the marks and indications of the souls of men, and while I endeavor by these to portray their lives, may be free to leave more weighty matters and great battles to be treated of by others."

But I say that Plutarch did treat of the most weighty matters, those being the hearts and characters of human beings, and that the things he says he will not account (although of course he does account them, in voluminous detail) are of much less weight. It is a matter of historical interest, for example, that Alexander hewed such a vast empire in so few years while so young, and his violent exploit certainly influences and informs modern boundaries and nations in Europe and the Near East; but what do we learn of Alexander by the record of the people he defeated, or by a careful accounting of the military means by which his victories were won? What do we learn of ourselves? That we are capable of ferocious ambition and murder, that we might commit any act for power and glory? This, from vast experience, we knew.

Plutarch, however, tells us of the desperately thirsty Alexander who refuses water because there is not enough for all his men—the same Alexander who in a drunken rage spears his friend Clitus through the heart for disagreeing with him; of the munificent Alexander who casually gave away a hundred fortunes to his soldiers, and the bloody Alexander who casually has a hundred prisoners killed to mark the festive occasion as he enters Asia; of the boy Alexander so temperate with bodily pleasures that "he was with much difficulty incited to them," and the man Alexander who was, says Plutarch bluntly, "addicted to drinking," and died of a roaring fever after a long bender; of the Alexander so little concerned with money that he gave away all his wealth to his soldiers, and so much concerned with fame that when abandoning a battlefield on the Ganges he deliberately left larger-than-life weapons and gear to be found and wondered over; of the Alexander so keenly sensitive of his status as future emperor that he would foot-race only with kings—the same Alexander who, at the height of his all-conquering fame, told his friends that if he were not the peripatetic lord of the known world, he would choose to be the penniless and sedentary philosopher Diogenes.

In short, Plutarch gives us the man's tumultuous heart, even as he chronicles the man's relentless march through life; and the richer tale, the one that truly educates, is of Alexander grappling not with the many nations and peoples he attacked, but with his own incendiary ambition, personal demons, and awful success.

In a sense, Plutarch is the first great modern writer, for while he is absorbed by the stories of great men (great Greek and Roman men only, actually, no Africans or Slavs or Teutons or Egyptians or other members of the Roman Empire need apply) as clues to character, he is more absorbed by their actions as revelation of the personal than as parable for the public, despite his avowals that the whole thesis of the *Lives* was moral uplift. "Using history as a mirror, I try somehow to improve my own life by modeling it upon the virtues of the men I write about," he wrote. "In the study of and writing of history, we receive in our souls memorials of the best. . . . This enables us to drive away and put far from us all the base or corrupt or ignoble influences produced by our associations with those with whom circumstances compel us to mingle. Thus we are enabled to discipline our thoughts and to direct them toward the finest examples of conduct."

I believe him about his motivation—he was a priest, after all, and a man utterly convinced that personal, civic, and religious virtue were the keystones of civilization—but I also think that he was too good a literary artist to be satisfied with sermonizing, and that while his overarching theme was the virtue of the moral life, the power and allure of his narrative was (and is) his fascination with character, the pressures that formed and revealed it, and the grace or lack thereof with which those pressures were endured.

Homer was after character too, to a degree—the *Odyssey* is in part certainly a character study of its hero, and a powerful image of Odysseus (broad sailor-shoulders, salt-cured face, hawk glare, hard head) stays with a reader for a lifetime. But Homer was primarily after the sweep of historical narrative, the ocean of saga, whereas Plutarch wanted to explore the immeasurable ocean of one man at a time. It may well be that Plutarch's great mission was to leave behind a series of moral lessons, a lively catechism—this is a man, after all, who also wrote a collection of homilies called the *Morals,* as well as three lost books about the soul—but the prime virtue of his *Lives* is not so much their moral uplift but their uncanny personality.

Plutarch's lost books, I note with heartfelt regret, include not only those three volumes on the soul but four books of commentaries on Homer, which certainly must be accounted among the lost treasures of Western criticism. Contemplating the whole awful list of his missing books (culled from a list of all Plutarch's works drawn up by his son Lamprias) is, as John Dryden noted, something like a merchant perusing a bill of freight after he has lost the ship that carried the goods. Among the literary creations no longer in the world, or hidden in crevices and cellars not yet unearthed, are Plutarch's eight books on Aristotle, six books of essays, four books on history, three books of fables, three books on sense, three books on justice, three books on cities, two books on politics, two books of proverbs, and lives of Hercules, Pindar, Augustus, Claudius, Nero, and Caligula, among others. The mind reels, partly at lost possibility—Plutarch on Augustus, what a match of fine emperor and fine essayist!—but more at the man's sheer industry, at the eye-popping range of his thought, and at the vagaries of history that cast off six books of Plutarch's essays while producing the muck that infests much of the modern bookshelf.

*  *  *

My own favorite of all Plutarch's *Lives* is his story of Antony, in which Plutarch's art rises to its zenith; for here he had a most remarkable man to explore, a peculiar man in whom swirled all sides of the human character, brave and craven at once, and all this courage and cowardice and lust and love is set against the most dramatic and colorful background imaginable—a battle between two mighty generals for the whole Roman Empire, a brilliant and power-hungry enchantress (Cleopatra), the betrayal of friends and nation—the whole nine yards of melodrama and B movies, absent only a swelling soundtrack and Technicolor. Plutarkos must have rubbed his hands with glee when it came time to tell of Antony.

"A very beautiful youth," he says of the boy Antony, "but by the worst of misfortunes, he fell into the acquaintance and friendship of Curio, a man abandoned to his pleasures, who plunged him into a life of drinking and dissipation. . . ." Antony, of an "ostentatious, vaunting temper, full of empty flourishes and unsteady efforts for glory," does what restless and reckless young men have always done as a desperate corrective—he joins the army, and pours all his yearning for fame and furious energy into battle.

He leads the Romans against the rebel Aristobolus and his Jewish army. He conquers Egypt, winning "a great name among the Alexandrians" by preventing a massacre of the losers (that great reputation in Egypt echoing in the ears of a young girl in Alexandria, Cleopatra), and becoming the rising Julius Caesar's right-hand man. By now, grown into his manhood, he has developed a great fame among the common soldiers for dressing, acting, and talking like them; achieved a reputation as a ladies' man (and "an ill name for familiarity with other people's wives"); and his "good humor, generous ways, his open and lavish hand in gifts and favors to his friends and fellow-soldiers, did a great deal for him in his first advance to power, and after he had become great, long maintained his fortunes, when a thousand follies were hastening their overthrow."

So sets the pattern of Antony's life: wonderfully brave and crafty in battle ("there was not one of the many engagements that now took place one after another in which he did not signalize himself"), and amazingly lazy and ill-mannered in private life ("his drinking bouts at all hours, his wild expenses, his gross amours, the day spent in sleeping or walking off his debauches, and the night in banquets and at theaters, and in celebrating the nuptials of some comedian or buffoon"). After Caesar is murdered in the senate, Antony vies with Caesar's nephew Octavian—later Augustus—for the empire, is defeated at Modena, and is forced to flee Italy.

But "it was his character in calamities to be better than at any other time," observes Plutarch. "Antony, in misfortune, was most nearly a virtuous man. It is common enough for people, when they fall into great disasters, to discern what is right, and what they ought to do; but there are but few who in such extremities have the strength to obey their judgment, either in doing what it approves or avoiding what it condemns; and a good many are so weak as to give way to their habits all the more, and are incapable of using their minds. Antony, on this occasion, was a most wonderful example to his soldiers. He, who had just quitted so much luxury and sumptuous living, made no difficulty now of drinking foul water and feeding on wild fruits and roots. Nay, it is related they ate the very bark of trees, and, in passing over the Alps, lived upon creatures that no one before had ever been willing to touch."

Eventually Antony returns in force to Italy and divides the empire with Augustus (who changed his name, speculates the historian Suetonius, to distinguish himself from his two sisters, *both* named Octavia). His fortunes restored, Antony slides headlong into debauch again, this time while traveling with his army through Asia. "Such being his temper," writes Plutarch, with a nearly audible sigh of frustration, "the last and crowning mischief that could befall him came in the love of Cleopatra," which would eventually "stifle and corrupt any elements that yet made resistance in him of goodness and a sound judgment."

Shakespeare, who leaned heavily on a translation of Plutarch in writing his *Antony and Cleopatra* in 1606, has this account of Cleopatra sailing into Antony's ken for the first time:

> The barge she sat in, like a burnished throne,
> Burned on the water: the poop was beaten gold;
> Purple the sails, and so perfumed that

The winds were love-sick with them; the oars were silver,
Which to the tune of flutes kept stroke and made
The water which they beat to follow faster,
As amorous of their strokes. For her own person,
It beggared all description: she did lie
In her pavilion, cloth-of-gold of tissue,
Over-picturing that Venus where we did see
The fancy outwork nature: on each side her
Stood pretty dimpled boys, like smiling Cupids
With diverse-colored fans, whose wind did seem
To glow the delicate cheeks which they did cool. . . .

(The same passage in Plutarch: "She came sailing up the river . . . in a barge with gilded stern and outspread sails of purple, while oars of silver beat time to the music of flutes and fifes and harps. She herself lay all along under a canopy of cloth of gold, dressed as Venus in a picture, and beautiful young boys, like painted Cupids, stood on each side to fan her. Her maids were dressed like sea nymphs and graces, some steering at the rudder, some working at the ropes. The perfumes diffused themselves from the vessel to the shore, which was covered with multitudes running out of the city to see the sight. . . .")

We know the tale from that point: their torrid love affair, Antony's waffling between love and glory, his final battle with Augustus for the world title, his ignominious abandoning of the fight at sea to follow like a puppy at Cleopatra's fleeing keel, his suicide, and Cleopatra's subsequent close embrace of the deadly asp. Shakespeare uses their melodramatic tale to make a story of tragic and powerful love; Plutarch, treating the love affair like a virus ("the mischief that had long lain still, the passion for Cleopatra, which better thoughts had seemed to have lulled and charmed into oblivion, upon his approach to Syria gathered strength again, and broke out into a flame . . ."), is characteristically fascinated by their characters or lack thereof—and not only Antony but Cleopatra. As clearly as he considers her Antony's bane, he cannot help but explore her charms, and delve into what it was that made her so mesmerizing not only to Antony but, before him, to Julius Caesar—two of the greatest men of her day. "For her actual beauty, it is said, was not in itself so remarkable that none could be compared with her, or that no one could see her without being struck by it, but the contact of her presence, if you lived with her, was irresistible; the attraction of her person, joining with the charm of her conversation, and the character that attended all she said or did, was something bewitching. It was a pleasure merely to hear the sound of her voice, with which, like an instrument of many strings, she could pass from one language to another; so that there were few of the barbarian nations that she answered by an interpreter; to most of them she spoke herself, as to the Ethiopians, Troglodytes, Hebrews, Arabians, Syrians, Medes, Parthians, and many others, whose language she had learnt; which was all the more surprising because most of the kings, her predecessors, scarcely gave themselves the trouble to acquire the Egyptian tongue. . . ."

Clearly a woman of many parts, who won back the throne of her country from usurping siblings at age seventeen, held it for twenty-two years, and died at thirty-nine by her own hand, bereft of the man she loved, and unwilling to be brought as prisoner to Rome, there to be exhibited, chained, in the traditional triumphant march of the conqueror. So passed Cleopatra, queen of the Nile.

Plutarch ends his tale with a dark note; among Antony's descendants was Claudius, who became emperor, and who adopted Lucius Domitius, "giving him the name Nero Germanicus," says Plutarch. "He was emperor in our time, and put his mother to death, and with his madness and folly came not far from ruining the Roman empire, being Antony's descendant in the fifth generation."

\* \* \*

Closing Plutarch after a long voyage among his tales, a reader is awash in a sea of images, the riveting human stories of men long dead brought to magical, immortal immediacy by one man with a relentless pen and sharp ear. Again and again Plutarch gives us a small gesture or remark or anecdote that gives us the whole tenor of the man: The great orator and statesman Cicero perceiving that his death was hard upon him in the persons of Antony's soldiers, and so commanding his servants to set down the litter in which they were carrying him to freedom, "and stroking his chin, as he used to do, with his left hand, he looked steadfastly upon his murderers, his person covered with dust, his hair and beard untrimmed, and his face worn with his troubles . . . and thus was he murdered, stretching forth his neck out of the litter, being now in his sixty-fourth year."

Sylla, who "when supreme master of all, was often wont to muster together the most impudent players and stage-followers of the town, and to drink and bandy jests with them without regard to his age or the dignity of his place."

Pericles, silent, "near his end," surrounded by his friends and family, who were "speaking of the greatness of his merit, and his power, and reckoning up his famous actions and the number of his victories," talking among themselves "as though he were unable to understand or mind what they said, but had now lost all his consciousness," but Pericles suddenly speaks up and "said that he wondered they should commend and take notice of things which were as much owing to fortune as to anything else, and had happened to many other commanders . . . and not speak or make mention of that which was the most excellent and greatest thing of all: 'no Athenian, through my means, ever wore mourning.'"

Marcius Coriolanus flipping off the hood that hides his face, as he sits at the hearth of Tullus, his bitterest enemy, and offering Tullus and the Volsicans his military skills against his native Rome—a breathtaking act of treason beginning on a stool by a crackling fire with the stroke of a man's hand against the cloth of his cloak. Calippus, architect of the murder of Dion, himself eerily later killed by the same Spartan-made sword ("the workmanship of it very curious," observes Plutarch meticulously). The Spartan king Agesilaus, who was "said to have been a little man, of a contemptible presence; but the goodness of his humor, and his constant cheerfulness and playfulness of temper, always free from anything of moroseness or haughtiness, made him more attractive, even to his old age, than the most beautiful and youthful men of the nation." The Athenians of Demosthenes' time going house to house, searching for stolen treasure, but leaving one house unsearched, that of a newly married couple, "out of respect to the bride who was within." Demosthenes himself, burning to be a great orator but physically "meagre and sickly," afflicted with "a perplexed and indistinct utterance and shortness of breath which by breaking and disjointing his sentences much obscured the sense and meaning of what he spoke," practicing speeches with pebbles in his mouth, and declaiming speeches and verses as he sprinted up hills, and building himself an underground chamber in which to practice for hours every day, "and here he would continue, oftentimes without intermission, for two or three months together, shaving one half of his head, that so for shame he might not go abroad, though he desired it ever so much." *Though he desired it ever so much!*—you can almost *taste* the boy's furious ambition, and see him sweating and shouting up the hills like a high-school football player preparing for two-a-day drills.

Antony, who "went out one day to angle with Cleopatra, and being so unfortunate as to catch nothing in the presence of his mistress, gave secret orders to the fishermen to dive under water, and put fishes that had already been taken upon his hooks." Sharp-eyed Cleopatra, seeing this dodge, arranging for a dried fish to be put on his hook, to the great laughter of onlookers. Tiberius Gracchus, fleeing his assassins "in his undergarment only," having thrown off his gown, at which his pursuers clutched as he sprinted through Rome—his death the first sedition to draw blood among the Romans since they had abandoned their kings centuries before. Artaxerxes of Persia, his right hand much bigger than his left. Aratus, at age seven, wandering the disordered streets of Sicyon as his father's killers search for him. Alexander, from whom "a most agreeable odor exhaled . . . his breath and body all over so fragrant as to perfume the clothes which he wore next him. . . ."

* * *

Yet as much as a reader's mind is crammed with the thousand characters who populate Plutarch, and agog at the breadth of his detailed and vibrant natural histories of their feats and failures, it increasingly wishes to know the stage manager himself, who is fully as interesting as any of his subjects. There are so many tantalizing clues to the man—the dozens of lost books, the length and nature of his time in the capital of the Empire (five years in Rome? forty? diplomat? scholar? no one knows), the extent of his travels, the fact that he kept with him at all times a commonplace book, in which he was often seen to be hurriedly scribbling anecdotes as they drifted by in conversations (Plutarkos, the Greek Boswell), his unusual predilection toward monotheism ("is not one Excellent Being, imbued with reason and intelligence, such as He whom we acknowledge to be the Father and Lord of all things, sufficient to direct and rule . . . ?"), his relations with Christianity (Plutarch "had heard of the Christian religion, and inserted several of its mysteries in his books," says the historian Theodoret—imagine a Plutarchian *Life of Paul*, Paul the prickly public relations genius who marketed Christ worldwide, or of Jesus himself—the Gospel according to Plutarch!), his relations with the emperors, especially Trajan, to whom Plutarch sent a legendarily taut, dry-witted recipe for empiring: "Let your government commence in your breast: and lay the foundation of it in the commands of your passions. If you make virtue the rule of your conduct, and the end of your actions, every thing will proceed in harmony and order. I have explained to you the spirit of those laws and constitutions that were established by your predecessors; and you have nothing to do but to carry them into execution. If this should be the case, I shall have the glory of having formed an emperor to virtue; but if otherwise, let this letter remain a testimony with succeeding ages, that you did not ruin the Roman empire under pretense of the counsels or the authority of Plutarch."

But, failing the discovery of his lost books, there is no way now of seeing more of the man, and we are left with his counsels and authority, which have been touchstones of Western literature and culture since he wrote them by the sea nineteen centuries ago. Ralph Waldo Emerson, a brilliant aphorist but dull essayist who must have gritted his teeth in envy at Plutarch's vibrant prose, had the character himself to sense that the Greek's work would never disappear ("Plutarch's popularity will return in rapid cycles. . . . His sterling values will recall the life and thought of the best minds, and his books will be reprinted and read anew by coming generations. And thus Plutarch will be perpetually rediscovered from time to time as long as books last"), but of all the compliments one might collect for Plutarch, I choose, as John Dryden did in an appendix to his translation of the Lives in 1686, one by Theodorus Gaza, "a man learned in the Latin tongue, and a great restorer of the Greek, who lived about two hundred years ago," says Dryden. "'Tis said that, having this extravagant question put to him by a friend, that if learning must suffer a general shipwreck, and he had only his choice left him of preserving one author, who should be the man, he would preserve, he answered, Plutarch; giving this reason, that in saving him he should secure the best collection of them all."

Theodorus had his hat on straight here, I think; and of all the literary geniuses in the West these last three millennia, the extraordinary men and women who reached into themselves to tell true of us all, the one in whom nearly all stories may be found is Plutarch. We do not know who Homer was—Samuel Butler famously thought Homer a brilliant young woman—and we are not at all sure who Shakespeare was, the glove-maker's son and the Earl of Oxford being the current arm-wrestlers for the name. But dimly across nineteen centuries we do see Plutarch the human being, and sense under his voluminous work the voluminous man, as complex and intricately threaded as any of his subjects: a dignified but warm husband and father, stern but affable neighbor, eloquent statesman and scholar, reverent priest, and most of all—best of all—a genius of a storyteller, a spinner of tales unsurpassed in our recorded literature.

For all his diligence as a scholar and historian digging after the details of the lives and characters of his subjects, Plutarch did spin some tales out of nearly whole cloth (Theseus and Romulus, for example), and he danced around the sparseness of fact with his usual graceful humor: "As geographers . . . crowd into the edges of their maps parts of the world which they do not know about, adding notes in the margin to the effect, that beyond this lies nothing but sandy deserts full of wild beasts, unapproachable bogs, Scythian ice, or a frozen sea, so, in this work of mine . . . after passing through those periods which probable reasoning can reach to and real history find a footing in, I might very well say of those that are farther off, Beyond this there is nothing but prodigies and fictions. . . . Let us hope that Fable may, in what shall follow, so submit to the purifying processes of Reason as to take the character of exact history. In any case, however, where it shall be found contumaciously slighting credibility, and refusing to be reduced to anything like probable fact, we shall beg that we may meet with candid readers, and such as will receive with indulgence the stories of antiquity."

So to resurrect this most interesting of our ancient cousins, as he resurrected so many others, we make a prodigy and fiction, and beg indulgence of candid readers, and bring Plutarkos closer to the camera, that we might see the literature of his face, and read a bit of his heart. Choose a happy day for the man, a summer day in his village—mid-September, perhaps, when the weather has just turned a corner and afternoons are russet at the edges, the days still hot but the nights brisk, the ocean darker by the day. Late in the afternoon in his cottage over the sea Plutarch is scribbling furiously—it's his *Life of Hercules* and it's going *very* well, it's nearly writing itself, everyone has a Hercules story to tell—but his hand is starting to cramp and he pauses, stands, stretches at length like his cat, looks casually out to sea. Something about the ocean this afternoon makes him lean out his window for a better look—maybe this was how the sea looked, wind-tossed and glittering, to Homer? Or to Odysseus . . . now *there* was a man who must have been able to read the moods and hours of the ocean like a book after twenty years at sea, hmm? . . . how would such water-wisdom form a man, I wonder . . . wouldn't he yearn to read faces that way too, trying to peer under the surface for the weather to come, for the hidden currents, for the shoals, for the jagged dangers?

His meditation is interrupted by two voices, wind-splintered by the growing breeze: wife Timoxena and daughter Timoxena, the child bounding like a deer into his view and laughing through the window *Father, Father, come out in the light! Come look for whales with me!* And he grins, does Plutarkos, unable to resist her verve and glee—the sheer energy of that child, she's got more pepper than all the boys combined!—and he steps out on the bright porch and savors the salt of the sea, the hot hand of the sun. He stands for a moment with his wife, their arms intertwined, clothes fluttering, daughter dancing in a circle and humming, and they talk of writing and dinner and her cousin in Athens and the foreman who probably did steal those tiles, and they talk about her health—she's been coughing so in the mornings, should they make that trip to Delphi now, or wait a bit?—and then little Timoxena trips over the edge of the table as she spins and she cuts her arm, *Father! it's bleeding!,* and he rocks her in his arms with her head in his chest until suddenly smiling shly slyly she says *will you walk on the beach with me before dark?* And he says yes of course my tiny flower and down the street they go to the sea, father and daughter, hand in hand, immortal.

CHAPTER FOUR

# A Head Full of Swirling Dreams

The man who was perhaps the finest writer ever in the English language was a ham-handed playwright, a less-than-minor poet, a fitful journalist, and the author of several awful novels. What might have been his crowning masterpiece was never finished; only a scrap of his most ambitious project was ever published; and he died young, just as his work was sharpening and deepening in startling ways.

Yet Robert Louis Balfour Stevenson, born in Scotland in 1850 and killed by a stroke as he made a salad for dinner at his house in Samoa, also wrote a timeless classic of young adult fiction (*Treasure Island*), two and a half other novels of the first rank (*Kidnapped, The Strange Case of Dr. Jeykll and Mr. Hyde,* and the unfinished *Weir of Hermiston*), a classic children's book of poems (*A Child's Garden of Verses*), and a first-rate travel book (*Travels with a Donkey in the Cévennes*).

He was additionally a fine essayist, a prescient political reporter (who predicted the fall of totalitarianism), a skilled social anthropologist, a maker of historical fiction in the vein of his countryman Sir Walter Scott, an early practitioner of modernist fiction (*The Beach of Falesá*), a sharp-eyed chronicler of nature and landscape, a biographer (of a beloved college professor), a historian (of Edinburgh), a prolific and hilarious letter writer, a composer of deft and poignant prayers, and even the author of popular horror stories (*The Merry Men*). He created a handful of characters who will live in the popular imagination and culture for centuries: the cunning and complex pirate Long John Silver, the dashing and vain Scottish rebel Alan Breck Stewart, the bipolar everyman Doctor Jekyll.

And all this in two decades: he was twenty-three when his first essay appeared in a magazine, twenty-eight when his first book was published (*An Inland Voyage*, his account of a canoe trip in France), thirty-three when *Jeykll and Hyde* made him world-famous, and only forty-four when he died in the South Seas.

Considering that the man threw fastballs in most every literary genre there is, and considering that none of the many writers of genius we know threw such high heat in so many ballparks, it seems to me we might account the grinning Scotsman with the tubercular cough and cigarette and stories always on his lips to be maybe the best writer our language has known; or at least the most comprehensively accomplished. That is a remarkable epitaph for a man who at age twenty-five was noted in his native Edinburgh mostly as a rake, failed lawyer, and "horrible atheist," as his shocked and devoutly Presbyterian parents said of their only child.

* * *

Stevenson wanted to be a writer before he could write. By age six he had dictated a history of Moses to his mother. By age ten he was inventing his own brief plays for a miniature theater he conducted with his cousin Bob. By age twelve he was playing "the sedulous ape" to Hazlitt, Lamb, Defoe, Hawthorne, Montaigne, Baudelaire, Chaucer, Ruskin, and Swinburne—by his own account immediately writing passages in their styles as soon as he finished one of their books.

> All through my boyhood and youth, I was known and
> pointed out for the pattern of an idler, and yet I was always
> busy on my own private end, which was to learn to write.
> I kept always two books in my pocket, one to read, one to
> write in. As I walked, my mind was busy fitting what I saw
> with appropriate words . . . [which] taught me (so far as
> I have learned them at all) the lower and less intellectual
> elements of the art, the choice of the essential note and
> the right word.

At age sixteen he wrote a brief history of the Pentland Rising, a Scottish revolt against England. At seventeen he enrolled at the University of Edinburgh, ostensibly to study engineering, the profession in which his father and uncles had earned national renown; the Stevensons were famed especially for their deft touch with lighthouses, beloved and crucial structures in a nation so rimed by rugged coast. But Louis, as his family called him to distinguish him from his exuberant cousin, was soon spending all his time in bars, brothels, and the shabby offices of the student debating society, where he spent his time arguing about literature and politics, and writing the ornate essays he would later collect as *Virginibus Puerisque.*

It was soon clear he was no engineer. His father insisted that he pursue an orthodox profession, and Louis dutifully passed his law examinations, was called to the bar, and admitted to the firm of Skene and Peacock in Edinburgh, for whom he practiced briefly and badly. In 1876 he embarked on a canoe trip through France with a friend, and very soon the law and the various travails of his life in Edinburgh faded away utterly, for in France he found his voice as a writer, found a climate more suitable than dank Scotland for his ravaged lungs, and found the love of his life—a married woman from a farming family in Indianapolis, Indiana.

\* \* \*

They met at the Hotel Chevillon in Grez. Fanny Vandergrift—Fanny Osbourne since her marriage at seventeen to an Army lieutenant—was thirty-six years old that summer, traveling with her son and daughter, separated from her repeatedly unfaithful husband, and mourning the recent death of her younger son. Grez was an artists' colony to which Fanny had repaired on her doctor's advice. Stevenson had visited thrice before with his cousin Bob. In July of 1876 Bob had preceded him to Grez, and there was much anticipation, among the painters and poets and interested Osbournes, of the arrival of Bob's wild cousin Louis.

A hot night, early that month; the bohemians are gathered for dinner at the large table in the hotel dining room; darkness falls as wine circulates and laughter rises. Then Fanny's son Lloyd, age eight, hears a noise outside, and an instant later a thin young man vaults lightly into the room through the window. Bob Stevenson stands and gravely announces the dusty man with the knapsack: "My cousin, Louis Stevenson."

Stevenson wrote later that he had stood long in the dark outside the window that night, staring at Fanny's face, instantly smitten; and as the scholar Richard Holmes has written dryly, "perhaps he did." Suffice it to say that Stevenson and Fanny were soon very much in love; and there is no question that Fanny's love sparked something great in Stevenson. From 1876 until his death eighteen years later, whether confined to bed or not, he was continually "darkly engaged with an ink-bottle," as he wrote to his friend Sidney Colvin.

In his last five years alone, perhaps the healthiest of his life, he wrote what the scholar J. C. Furnas estimated to be 700,000 published words—about a dozen books' worth of prose, poetry, prayers, and politics. His collected works, published posthumously, ran to thirty-five volumes.

* * *

He and Fanny courted each other for the next three years, in France and then in America, which Stevenson crossed by train on the way to meet Fanny in San Francisco. (Of Nebraska he wrote with amazement, "We were at sea—there is no other adequate expression. . . . To one hurry-ing through by steam there was a certain exhilaration in this spacious vacancy, this greatness of the air, this discovery of the whole arch of heaven, this straight, unbroken, prison-line of the horizon.") Fanny finally procured her divorce in 1879, and Mr. Stevenson and the former Miss Vandergrift were married in San Francisco in 1880, when he was twenty-nine and she forty.

They honeymooned in Napa Valley, where Stevenson observed a nascent wine industry with a connoisseur's interest ("imperial elixirs, beautiful to every sense, gem-hued, flower-scented, dream-compellers") and began a consideration of California, *The Silverado Squatters,* in which he foresaw the future timber wars: "California has been a land of promise in its time, like Palestine; but if the woods continue so swiftly to perish, it may become, like Palestine, a land of desolation. We may look forward to a time when there will not be [a tree] left standing in that land . . . man in his short-sighted greed robs the country of the noble redwood. Yet a little while and perhaps all the hills of seaboard California may be bald."

The Stevensons then set about over the next six years trying to find a beneficent climate for Louis, whose health continued to plummet. They tried Switzerland, Scotland (where he began *Treasure Island* one rainy day after idly drawing a map of the island to amuse his stepson), England (where he became dear friends with Henry James and wrote *Jekyll and Hyde* in a week), and finally New York, where he spent an afternoon talking in Washington Square with Mark Twain and a dark icy winter at Saranac Lake in the Adirondacks—which provided him the dark brooding background for much of the dark brooding novel *The Master of Ballantrae.*

But America proved no better for his health than Europe had, and finally, perhaps in desperation and certainly with a devil-may-care sense that he had better savor life while he could ("I wish to die in my boots . . . no more Land of Counterpane for me"), Louis and his family chartered a private schooner and set out from San Francisco to the South Seas. It was June 28, 1888—a dozen years since he'd leaped lightly through the hotel window at Grez. The *Casco* stopped briefly in San Francisco Bay, for last letters to be dropped into a tugboat, and then off it sailed into the Pacific, from which Robert Louis Stevenson—by now the most famous author in the world, courtesy of *Jekyll and Hyde*, which had been an immediate sensation—would never return.

* * *

During those dozen years in sickbeds all over Europe he had been furiously busy—busier, perhaps, than he might have been healthy, for when upright and surrounded by visitors he was a talker of legendary wit and range. A family friend remembered the first time she heard his voice: "Suddenly from out of a dark corner came a voice peculiar, vibrating . . . I listened in perplexity and amazement. Who was this . . . who talked as Lamb wrote? This young Heine with a Scottish accent? I stayed long, and when I came away the unseen converser came down with me to the front door . . . I saw a slender, brown, long-haired lad with great dark eyes, a brilliant smile. . . ."

It was Stevenson at age seventeen.

"Grave argument and criticism, riotous streaks of fancy, flashes of nonsense more illuminating than wisdom, streamed from him inexhaustibly as he kindled with delight at the delight of his hearers . . . 'til all of us seemed to catch something of his own gift and inspiration," remembered his dear friend Sir Sidney Colvin. "As long as he was there you kept discovering with delight unexpected powers in yourself. . . . He was a fellow of infinite and unrestrained jest and yet of infinite earnest, the one very often a mask for the other."

Stevenson characteristically wrote beautifully of talking:

> There can be no fairer ambition than to excel in talk; to be affable, gay, ready, clear and welcome. . . . Literature in many of its branches is no other than the shadow of good talk; but the imitation falls far short of the original in life, freedom, and effect. . . . Talk is fluid, tentative, continually in further

search and progress; while written words remain fixed,
become idols even to the writer, found wooden dogmatisms,
and preserve flies of obvious error in the amber of the truth
... [talk] is the scene and instrument of friendship, the
gauge of relations, the sport of life. ... True talk, that strikes
out the slumbering best of us, is founded as deep as love in
the constitution of our being, and is a thing to relish with all
our energy, while yet we have it.

He loved to talk and he loved fine wine (he had casks of French
wine shipped to him in Samoa) and he loved his native land, despite
his voluntary exile from it to the other end of the world; he returned
to Scotland again and again in his work, setting *Kidnapped* (and its
dull sequel, *Catriona*), part of *The Master of Ballantrae*, and all of
*Weir of Hermiston* there. He had always "a strong Scottish accent of
the mind," as he said. "A Scottish child hears much of shipwreck ...
pitiless breakers, and great sea-lights; much of heathery mountains,
wild clans ... and the ring of foraying hoofs. He glories in his hard-
fisted forefathers, of the iron girdle and the handful of oatmeal, who
rode so swiftly and lived so sparely on their raids. Poverty, ill-luck,
enterprise, and constant resolution are the fibres of the legend of his
country's history."

\* \* \*

The *Casco* was many thousands of miles from Scotland and a
month out of San Francisco when Stevenson saw, at dawn, the sight
he had longed for since boyhood. "The first love, the first sunrise,
the first South Sea island, are memories apart and touched a virgin-
ity of sense," he wrote. "Slowly [the Marquesas] took shape in the
attenuating darkness ... like the pinnacles of some ornate and monstrous church, they stood there, in the sparkling brightness of the
morning, the fit signboard of a world of wonders."

And wonderful the whole of the South Seas turned out to be for
him; his health improved to the point where he could walk and ride
for hours, and putter about in his woods and gardens until joyously
exhausted, and spend his time (when not writing notes for the vast
book he wanted to make on the South Seas), "cutting about the
world loose, like a grown-up person."

From Nukahiva they sailed to the Paumotus, Tahiti, and Hawaii,
where Stevenson finished *The Master of Ballantrae* and sipped

champagne with Kalakaua, the last king of Hawaii, who had read *Treasure Island* and *Jekyll and Hyde*. Louis also visited the leper colony at Molokai, made famous by the late Belgian priest Father Damien who who had devoted his life to it. This week-long visit led to what the scholar Ian Bell calls "one of the most sustained, comprehensive, delicate, penetrating and vicious pieces of invective in the language," Stevenson's icily furious "An Open Letter to the Reverend Dr. Hyde." Hyde (the coincidence of the name is startling) was a stuffy Protestant minister who had "publicly accused Damien of vice and incompetence, and of being "coarse, dirty, headstrong, bigoted . . . [and] not a pure man in his relations with women . . . the leprosy of which he died should be attributed to his vices and carelessness."

Stevenson's passionate reply, initially privately circulated for sensible fear of a libel suit, punctured the sanctimonious Hyde, defended the memory of "so much better a man than you or me," and was soon reprinted around the world. Stevenson refused all payment (which would be "cannibalism," he said) for its appearances, and had proceeds from it, as well as a piano, sent to Molokai.

Next the Stevensons sailed to what are now the Gilbert Islands (then the Kingsmills), where they discovered the entire population of Great Makin Island drunk after a Fourth of July bash; met the legendary King Tembinoka of Apemama, who wore dresses and military uniforms alternately, and had long talks with Stevenson about law and medicine; and finally, on the morning of December 7, 1889, landed on Upolu, the largest of the Samoan islands (once called the Navigators), where Stevenson would live the rest of his brief life. The climate salved his lungs, and nearly as important, there was monthly mail service to San Francisco, by which means he could conduct his freelance work.

The Reverend Clarke of the London Missionary Society remembered meeting Louis and his wife and stepson minutes after they'd landed in Samoa, at Apia, the harbor town: Fanny with a straw hat and a guitar over her shoulder, Lloyd with a banjo on his back and huge gold earrings, and Louis barefoot and "dressed in a shabby suit of white flannels that had seen many better days, a white yachting cap, and a cigarette in his mouth." Clarke, who was to become a good friend of the Stevensons, reported that he mistook this colorful crew for itinerant musicians or thespians on their way to New Zealand.

\* \* \*

Samoa in 1889 was controlled by England, Germany, and the United States, who were interested in establishing missions, plantations, and trading routes, respectively. The native king, Mataafa, had been deposed by the Germans for the unpardonable act of defeating German troops. Stevenson dove headlong into Samoan politics, becoming so embroiled that he was in danger of being deported by the angry Germans, and he became a trusted friend of the Samoans, who called him Tusitala, the teller of tales, and built him a road from the harbor to his house in gratitude for his support.

Soon he was also a Samoan landowner, buying some four hundred acres of highland forest for about four hundred pounds, and the whole motley retinue (Louis, Fanny, and Lloyd; Fanny's daughter Belle and her husband and son; and, eventually Stevenson's mother) settled muddily at what Stevenson called Vailima, or Five Waters. "We . . . have five streams, waterfalls, precipices, profound ravines, rich tablelands . . . a great view of forest, sea, mountains, the warships . . . really a noble haven," he wrote to a friend.

Here, for five years, with interruptions only for brief voyages to Sydney and Honolulu, Stevenson wrote ten books (among them *A Footnote to History*, his account of the troubles in Samoa), and reveled in the best health of his life. "It is like a fairy story that I should have recovered health and strength, and should go round again among my fellow-men, boating, riding, bathing, toiling hard with a wood-knife in the forest . . . Nothing is so interesting as weeding, clearing, and path-making," wrote Louis. Beset by writer's cramp, he often dictated his work to his stepdaughter Belle, who was amazed at his ability to invent without ever faltering for a word. The stories poured out—novels, poems, travel writing. Many were left unfinished at his death; he liked to have several projects going at once, leaping from one to another as his interest waxed and waned, as the scholar Philip Callow notes.

Some of these works were "machines," as Stevenson himself described one to Henry James. But two were first rate: *The Beach of Falesá* ("the first realistic South Sea story," wrote Louis, "I mean with real South Sea characters, and details of life") and the book he called *The Justice-Clerk*, published posthumously in 1896 as *Weir of Hermiston*. (Weir is the family name of the leading characters, and Hermiston is their family seat in the Scottish countryside.) In *Weir* his art rose to a new pitch—drawing together his beloved Scottish countryside and history with a heroine (Kirstie Elliott) who for once was a real character, passionate, complex, contradictory, and far more than the plot devices which his female characters had been in the past. As Callow notes, there are no women at all in *Treasure Island, Kidnapped,* and *Jekyll and Hyde. Weir* was something else altogether, and many a reader, male and female alike, has mourned its truncation. "A novel of far richer content," wrote the novelist Lettice Cooper in 1947, "remarkable not only for the power and grace of the execution, but for the brooding sense of destiny which gives it the quality of a Greek tragedy."

\* \* \*

The year 1894 was difficult for Stevenson. He worried about money; he'd sunk many thousands of dollars into his estate in an effort to make it a working planatation, to no avail. He was financially and emotionally responsible not only for his large family but for a dozen Samoan servants and workers whom he treated as extended clan. He owed thousands of dollars to local white traders, who overcharged him mercilessly, thinking him wealthy. Fanny was veering uneasily close to madness. Louis, painfully aware that finished books from his pen could earn instant healthy sums from American and European publishers, worked incessantly, and among his letters and remarks that year are dark notes from a man who had smiled through a lifetime of pain.

On New Year's Day he said "that he was too tired to work any more for six months at least," notes Callow. Later he told one friend that he wished for death, another that all was disillusion and defeat. "My skill deserts me," he wrote to Colvin in October, "such as it is, or was. It was a very little dose of inspiration, and a pretty little trick of style, long lost, improved by the most heroic industry . . . I am a fictitious article and have long known it. I am read by journalists, by my fellow novelists, and by boys."

On his birthday, November 13, the family savored a feast that included tinned salmon and champagne chilled with ice from a steamer in the harbor. "Dear Lou, what cause for thankfulness that he has been spared to see this birthday in so much health and comfort," wrote his mother in her diary. Similarly they feasted at a Thanksgiving dinner complete with roast turkey, sherry, Madeira, and Bordeaux.

On December 3, wrote Belle in her diary, "we worked steadily til nearly twelve, and then he walked up and down the room talking to me of his work, of future chapters, of bits of his past life that bore on what he had been writing—as only he could talk." Stevenson lunched with his friend Bazett Haggard (the novelist Rider Haggard's brother), the British land commissioner on the island, and then joined Belle's son Austin in cheerfully "making a great noise over their French lesson" on the verandah. Repairing to the kitchen to help Fanny make dinner, he found her morose; she'd had premonitions of disaster. To cheer her up he played a game of cards and fetched a bottle of Burgundy from the cellar.

And then, while helping with the salad, "he suddenly said 'What's that?' or 'What a pain!' and put both hands to his head," wrote Belle. "'Do I look strange?' he asked, and then he reeled and fell backwards. His favorite boy Sosimo caught him and carried him into the big room, and he was never conscious after . . . as the room darkened one by one all the Samoans on the place crept in silently and sat on the floor in a wide semi-circle around him . . . the night air came in scented with gardenias . . . he breathed fainter and at longer intervals until at last he died at ten minutes past eight."

His Samoan servants and neighbors, records Belle, "sat silent, bowed and reverent," and then chanted the Catholic prayers of the dead for their friend before slipping out and working all night cutting a path through the woods to the flat summit of Mount Vaea, "no bigger than a room," where they dug Tusitala's grave. In the afternoon his hand-carved coffin was carried to the summit and laid to rest. The Reverend Clarke conducted an Anglican service, and among the prayers recited that afternoon, high on a hill over the ocean, were prayers that Louis had written and recited to his family every evening.

Next day the chiefs of Samoa forbade the use of firearms on Mount Vaea, so that the birds and animals "might live undisturbed, and raise about his grave the songs he knew so well." Three years later a large cement tomb was raised over his grave. On the tomb there are bronze plates with bas reliefs of a thistle and a hibiscus flower (the characteristic plants of Scotland and Samoa), and Stevenson's famous poem "Requiem":

Under the wide and starry sky
Dig the grave and let me lie.
Glad did I live and gladly die
And I laid me down with a will.
This be the verse you grave for me:
'Here he lies where he longed to be;

Home is the sailor, home from sea,
And the hunter home from the hill.'

Fanny lived for another two decades, testily defending Louis's reputation against an honest biography (the first, by Stevenson's cousin Graham Balfour, is warm hagiography) and minding various revised editions and last works, among them the unfinished *In the South Seas* and *Weir of Hermiston,* both of which were printed in 1896. She sold Vailima in 1897, and the house on which and in which Louis had labored so became in turn the German governor's, the British governor's, the American governor's, and the presidential mansion of the independent Republic of Western Samoa. Today it is owned by Mormon missionaries and it serves as a Stevenson museum and tourist stop. (There are also Stevenson museums in Calistoga, Edinburgh, Saranac, and Monterey.)

His early death only cemented the romantic melodrama of Stevenson's life, and his legend—"the Dying Wanderer," sneered Christopher Isherwood—long overshadowed serious consideration of his work, despite such eloquent defenders as Henry James, G. K. Chesterton, Gerard Manley Hopkins, and Jorge Luis Borges. His virtues as a craftsman are summed ably by James ("Character is what he has . . . [and] a singular maturity of expression that he has given to young sentiments") and Chesterton, who lauded the clarity and verve of Louis's prose ("all his images stand out in sharp outline; and are, as it were, all edges. . . . The very words carry the sound and the significance. It is as if they were cut out with cutlasses."). But not until biographies by David Daiches (1947) and J. C. Furnas (1952) did Stevenson the artist of startling range begin to emerge from the colorful legend that had made him little more than "the patron saint of boys' adventures," as Ian Bell wrote.

Stevenson has flaws, of course: his female characters are generally shadows and stock pieces, he is subject to long languors, and the novels written with his stepson Lloyd Osbourne are worth reading only to try to catch Stevenson flitting in and out of the generally wooden prose. An an essayist he is liable to homilies and sermons, as a playwright forgettable, as a poet slight except for the one perfect book and a handful of lovely elegies, and the fiction he did not set in islands British or Pacific is forced (*Prince Otto,* for example).

Yet in his Pacific years he finally pared away mannerism and airy throwaway in his work; his essays tautened, his fiction opened to include well-drawn women for the first time, and his nonfiction, particularly the travel accounts collected as *In the South Seas,* brought all his novelist's gifts to bear on island kings, criminals, and politics, especially the crushing effect of imperialism on vulnerable cultures. That might have been his greatest subject in the end, for he dearly loved Samoa and Samoans, and saw very clearly that what was happening on his chosen island was happening around the world.

"You don't know what news is, nor what politics, nor what the life of man, till you see it on so small a scale and with your own liberty on the board for stake," he wrote to Henry James in 1892, while a savage little war raged in Samoa and he was likely to be imprisoned or deported. "I would not have missed it for much. And anxious friends beg me to stay at home and study human nature in Brompton drawing-rooms!"

But his epic account of imperialism and the death of native culture in the Pacific was never finished, as his great Scottish novel was never finished, because he who had been near death a dozen times in life died barely into his middle age. But he left varied greatness behind him: pulsing, vibrant, charming, passionate, exuberant novels, poems, travelogue, and essays that will live for centuries. Some of that work, like *Treasure Island* and the *Child's Garden of Verses,* is laudably passed from parents to children aloud, but much is also thrillingly found by young readers on their own, those lucky children who open Stevenson and walk with Jim Hawkins or David Balfour into a hair-raising adventure that has long outlived, and blessedly will continue to long outlive, the lively thin Scotsman who invented those tales long ago, stretched out in his bed with a pen and paper and cigarette and a head full of swirling dreams.

CHAPTER FIVE

# A Note on Allan Quatermain

In December of 1884 a young man named Henry Haggard was
riding into London on a train with one of his six brothers. The
two young men were talking about the most popular book in the
English-speaking world that year, Robert Louis Stevenson's *Treasure
Island*.

Haggard, according to his daughter Lilias years later, said he
didn't think *Treasure Island* was so very remarkable.

"I'd like to see you write anything half as good—bet you a bob you
can't," said his indignant brother.

"Done!" exclaimed Haggard.

When the train arrived he walked to his law office and began a
"book for boys," as he called it, that has since sold millions of
copies, inflamed the imaginations of millions of readers, and
sparked the young man's colorful literary career, a protean adventure
that produced sixty-eight books, essentially created the eternally
flourishing and morphing sword-and-sorcery and lost-city genres,
and directly influenced Rudyard Kipling, Edgar Rice Burroughs, and
J. R. R. Tolkien, and their countless successors in fiction, films,
comics, and computer games. To the twenty-eight-year-old Henry
Rider Haggard, then, ducking his work in the Probate and Divorce
Courts to write an adventure novel, we can assign credit—or affix
blame—for a vast chunk of modern pop culture.

The book that Haggard finished on April 21 of 1885 was *King
Solomon's Mines*. It was immediately rejected by the publishers
Hurst and Blackett, who had printed Haggard's first two unsuccess-
ful novels. The publishing firm Cassell's took the new book with
alacrity, however, mostly because of the vociferous admiration of
two of Robert Louis Stevenson's best friends, the critics and authors
Andrew Lang and W. E. Henley.

Haggard was offered a hundred pounds for the book, or fifty
pounds against future royalties. Having earned pennies from his

writing thus far, and with a wife and three children at home, Haggard chose the hundred pounds. Then came a Dickensian twist, as Haggard recalled in his memoirs: "As it chanced, however, there sat in the corner of the room a quiet clerk, whom I had never even noticed. When the editor had departed this unobtrusive gentleman addressed me. 'Mr Haggard,' he said in a warning voice, 'if I were you I would take the other agreement.' Then, hearing some noise, once more he became absorbed in his work, and I understood that the conversation was not to be resumed."

Haggard took the hint and the royalties, a decision that earned him a fortune for the rest of his days; although as he realized later to his bitter regret, he had also signed away the copyright, which Cassell's guarded closely until its expiration in 1975. Cassell's itself sold 30,000 copies in a year (aided in large part by the development in 1885 of both Linotype and Monotype typesetting machines), and 650,000 more copies in the next four decades, in addition to permitting many other editions. In the United States, where copyright piracy was the norm in 1885, thirteen unauthorized editions appeared within a year of the book's publication.

Haggard's moment with the quiet clerk was on May 29—five weeks after he recorded in his notebook that he had finished "Solomon's Mines 77,400 words (about)." On July 17 he started the sequel, this one named for the quiet hero of both books, *Allan Quatermain*. Haggard finished *Allan Quatermain* in ten weeks, on September 28—the day before Cassell's unveiled an eerily twenty-first-century advertising blitz. After dark on September 29, agents from Cassell's slapped long narrow posters up all over London with this meek encomium: KING SOLOMON'S MINES—THE MOST AMAZING BOOK EVER WRITTEN. The book arrived at bookstores the next morning. In the succeeding days it was lauded in *The Spectator, The Saturday Review, Vanity Fair, Public Opinion,* and *The Athenaeum* (which compared the fight scenes to those in Homer and Dumas), and Andrew Lang alone wrote twenty anonymous glowing reviews for it. Haggard's fame was launched.

In the next six months he wrote two more novels, *Jess* and *She,* the latter of which has also sold millions of copies, and like *King Solomon's Mines* was also eventually made into a popular movie (starring Ursula Andress, who inflamed the imaginations of boys more than any novel could). In the space of fourteen months, Haggard had written four novels, two of which are among the most popular books in history. In the annals of productive literary stretches, this must be accounted one of the great bursts—superseded in his own time only by the very man Haggard had so wanted to best to win a bet: Robert Louis Stevenson, who wrote *A Child's Garden of Verses, The Strange Case of Dr. Jekyll and Mr. Hyde,* and *Kidnapped* in the years 1885 and 1886.

\* \* \*

Of all Haggard's characters the most famous is Ayesha, the immortal She, queen of a mysterious and remote African kingdom and the one human being in history who has defeated death and lived for thousands of years; but for me the most enduring and interesting and accessible character is the quiet hunter Allan Quatermain, who Haggard wrote was "only myself set in a variety of imagined situations, thinking my thoughts and looking at life through my eyes." (Although, as Haggard's biographer D. S. Higgins noted gently, many of Haggard's British readers also saw a man named F. C. Selous, author of *A Hunter's Wanderings in Africa,* in the Quatermain character, and Haggard often spoke with admiration of the elderly adventurers he had known in his years in Africa.)

Whatever his provenance, Allan Quatermain's appeal is his reality—he is no cartoon or enfleshed idea but a man, with flaws he admits and flaws he doesn't see, with quiet courage and a quiet self-deprecating humor, with a spoken skepticism and an unspoken powerful faith in the persistence of love. He is Haggard's greatest creation because he doesn't seem created at all. His adventures, some quite wild, are recounted in an even tone, and much of the pleasure of the fourteen novels and four stories Haggard wrote about him comes from the fact that Allan is the modest reporter of his travels—which, given his calm character and professional gravitas, ostensibly precludes melodrama and gives the books a friendly, informative tone. They read like long, fascinating letters from a friend. "I, Allan, the most practical and unimaginative of persons, just a homely, half-educated hunter and trader who chances to have seen a good deal of the particular little world in which his lot was cast. . . ."

Allan is elderly as we meet him—"fifty-five last birthday," as he says in the first line of *King Solomon's Mines,* and "a small, withered, yellow-faced man of sixty three" in *Allan Quatermain.* He's thin—"nine stone six" in his clothes, or about 130 pounds. He limps from a lion bite in his thigh. His hair is grizzled and "stands up like a half-worn scrubbing brush." Thin hands, large brown eyes. Very good with horses and a deadly shot with any sort of rifle. Interested and able at languages; by the age of twenty he could speak English, Dutch, and four African dialects. Physically, despite his slightness, "a great deal tougher than the majority of men . . . nothing seemed to tire me. I could bear any amount of exposure and privation, and I never met the native who was my master in feats of endurance. Of course, all that is different now, I am speaking of my early manhood."

Son of a curate in Oxfordshire. Mother and three brothers dead of fever when he was a child; he and his missionary father removed to "Southern Africa" in an unspecified year in the latter nineteenth century. Married at age nineteen to Marie Marais, who sacrifices her life for his. Married at age twenty-four or so to Stella Carson, who bears their only child, Harry, before she too dies tragically young— as will Harry in his young manhood, while training to be a doctor. Allan never marries again over his next four decades, though he falls in love with a Zulu woman (Mameena, the Wailing Wind), and falls briefly under the romantic sway of two queenly white women, She and Nyleptha, whose beauty and power are such as to command infatuation from any man. (Haggard had a bit of a thing for the White Goddess figure, and one wonders at his influence on Robert Graves' curious mythology.)

An orderly man, Allan—suspicious of the influence of money, absorbed by the Old Testament, classic literature, and an obscure epic British poem called the Ingoldsby Legends; a great admirer of trees, a great hater of cockroaches, a man "intensely interested in past civilizations and their relics," interested in the religion and myth and wizardry of African cultures but avowedly skeptical, even of his friend the dwarf Zulu magician Zikali—Opener of Roads, Keeper of the Great Medicine, the Thing That Should Never Have Been Born.

An active man, from his youth to his very last days—"rest is good," he says in the course of his journey toward Ayesha's far country, "but for a man who has always led an active life, too much of it is very bad, for then he begins to think, and thought in large doses is depressing." A peaceful man "who loves quiet and home," but brave and calm in a fight. Prone to a grinning self-deprecation: "Most of us do more foolish things than wise ones and sometimes I think that in spite of a certain reputation for caution and far-sightedness, I am exceptionally cursed in this respect." (A self-analysis belied by the names given him by his Zulu companions: Macumazahn, the

Watcher by Night, he whose sharp eyes for danger are never closed; and, in a cheerful parade of epithets from a Zulu friend: "mighty chief! eater-up of lions, clever one! watchful one! brave one! quick one! whose shot never misses, who strikes straight home, who is a true friend . . .") For all his skepticism and urge to privacy, Allan is a man sensitive to duty, and willing to bear a heavy load when presented: "woe betide him who neglects his duty . . . I was appointed to try to hook a few fish out of the vast kettle of human woe, and go on hooking."

\* \* \*

In July of 1875 Rider Haggard had sailed for South Africa as a staffer for Sir Henry Bulwer, the new Lieutenant-Governor of Natal. Haggard was then nineteen years old, tall and thin, dreamy and sensitive, "too serious and gloomy for my age," thought by some to be conceited but perhaps trying to put a confident face on the youngest and least-accomplished member of the English party. To that point Haggard had proven himself in England to be a bad student, a mediocre athlete, and a "dull youth" of singularly unpromising prospects, according to his grim father, who had asked Bulwer to take on the boy as unpaid aide-de-camp.

The party stopped in Cape Town, steamed around the Cape to Durban, and then proceeded to Maritzburg, the British capital of Natal. Here Haggard embarked on his duties, such as they were (mostly arranging parties), but with such light work he had a great deal of time to explore Natal and its people, the Zulus. He studied them in person, "bronze-coloured, noble-looking, living in their kraals [corrals] filled with round beehive-like huts." He scoured official reports, he pumped old Natal hands for stories. In early 1876 he saw a Zulu war-dance, which occasioned his first published prose, an article in *The Gentleman's Magazine* in 1877.

By virtue of his position as staffer to the Governor, Haggard was also plunged into England's abrupt annexation of Natal's northern neighbor, the Transvaal, an ostensibly Boer possession but much contested, naturally enough, by the resident Zulu. When, in late 1876, an official English party was sent to Pretoria to formally annex the Transvaal, Haggard went along on the seven-week expedition through the bush, keeping a careful and detailed diary, meeting the Zulu warrior he would later make famous in the Allan stories (using his real name, Umslopogaas), and absorbing uncounted stories of battles, hunts, myths, murders, legends, and bush magic. He also narrowly missed being murdered by a Zulu army and was the Englishman who read aloud the annexation pronouncement in Pretoria's central marketplace

In 1877 Haggard was named assistant to the Transvaal's only judge, and spent the next two years, on and off, traveling the bush with the judge, living in a wagon drawn by eight oxen, armed with rifles and shotguns, visiting remote settlements of both races, and passing through the wonders of a country Haggard all the rest of his life called the most beautiful in the world—vast mountains, deep caves, endless herds of wildebeest, prides of lions not yet convinced by guns that they were not the top of the food chain. "Often and often I have crept shivering on to my waggon-box just as the sun rose and looked out," he wrote later. "At first one would see nothing but a vast field of white mist suffused toward the east by a tremulous golden glow, through which the tops of stony koppies [hills] stood up like gigantic beacons. From the dense mist would come strange sounds—snorts, gruntings, bellows, and the thunder of countless hoofs. Presently this great curtain would grow thinner, then it would melt, as the smoke from a pipe melts into the air, and for miles on miles the rolling country interspersed with bush opened to the view. But it was not tenantless as it is now, for as far as the eye could reach it was literally black with game."

Haggard also volunteered for the English cavalry in 1877, as tensions rose among English, Boer, and Zulus in Natal, and was elected lieutenant of the Pretoria Horse. But by 1879 it was clear to him and many others that the British Empire would soon abandon the Transvaal to the restless Boers and Zulus; Haggard's great love back in England, Lilly Jackson, had married another man; and so, discouraged on several fronts, he sailed home that summer. He would return once, briefly, with his new wife Louisa, to try farming and ostrich-ranching in Natal, but by 1881 he and his wife and new son Jock were back in England, where Haggard would spend the rest of his years. All told he had been five years in Africa—from which rich experience he would make many dozens of books and create the thin, quiet, grizzled hunter Allan Quatermain.

\* \* \*

Having invented Allan (or borrowed him from Selous) for *King Solomon's Mines,* Haggard killed him convincingly at the end of the sequel, and was forced to tell back-tales for the rest of the series. The scholar Douglas Melville has arranged the eighteen Allan stories in "Allan order"—the order in which the stories told occur in Allan's life. By this measurement *Allan's Wife* (1889) begins the saga with his birth and boyhood. Next comes *Marie* (1912), which accounts Allan's first adventures and the years from youth to young man. Then *Child of Storm* (1913), the 1887 short story "A Tale of Three Lions" (in which Allan explains why he limps), *Maiwa's Revenge* (1888), the stories "Hunter Quatermain's Story" and "Long Odds" (1885 and 1886, respectively), *The Holy Flower* (1915), *Heu-Heu* (1924), the 1921 novel She and Allan (in which the immortal Ayesha decides not to bother falling in love with such a leathery old hunter), *The Treasure of the Lake* (1926), *The Ivory Child* (1916), *Finished* (1917), the story "Magepa the Buck" (1912), and the novel that actually began it all, *King Solomon's Mines*. In the fictional years between that book and its sequel *Allan Quatermain,* in which the saga closes, Haggard later crammed in two more novels, *The Ancient Allan* (1920) and *Allan and the Ice-Gods* (1927), both of which are Allan's memoirs of previous incarnations, neither of which is very good, and the latter of which, like *The Treasure of the Lake,* was published after Haggard's own saga concluded with his death in 1925.

Reincarnation and life after death were two prime Haggard themes, as were, in no particular order, queenly white goddesses, bloody melees, lost cities, the brief and essentially impossible tenure of true love on this sweet green earth, severed limbs, the fine line between human beings and other mammals (his character Hendrika, the Baboon Woman in *Allan's Wife,* is a direct ancestor of Kipling's Mowgli), the fine line between life and death ("the veil between that what we see and the great invisible truths, the whisper of whose wings at times we hear as they sweep through the gross air of the world"), and the courage and character of Zulu people; this last a rare stance for a white man of his time.

Haggard's black characters, based on actual men and women, were not only completely human but often braver and more heroic than the white characters, often in defense of their land and patrimony, a stance Haggard championed, again relatively alone. ("I could never discern a superiority so great in ourselves as to authorise us, by right divine as it were, to destroy the coloured man and take his lands.") The king of these heroic black characters in his work is Umslopogaas, who in real life *was* kingly—he was the son of Mswazi, King of Swaziland. Haggard so admired him that

Umslopogaas got his own novel, *Nada the Lily*, which explains his early life and how he came by his huge rhinoceros-horn-handled axe, "the most remarkable and fatal hand-to-hand weapon I ever saw, which he seemed to look upon as an intimate friend, and to which he would sometimes talk by the hour, going over all his old adventures with it, and dreadful enough some of them were," remarks Allan. "By a piece of grim humour he had named this axe 'Inkosi-kass,' which is the Zulu word for chieftainess. For a long while I could not make out why he gave it such a name, and at last I asked him, when he informed me that the axe was evidently feminine, because of her womanly habit of prying very deep into things, and that she was clearly a chieftainess because all men fell down before her . . . [and] she must needs be wise, having 'looked into so many people's brains.'"

The driving engine of the Allan stories is action, usually a quest liberally salted with mayhem, all given the dusty cast of historical reality by Allan's matter-of-fact reportage. Yet Haggard, who might fairly be called a "pulp writer" though much of his work predated the birth of pulp journals in 1896, was quite capable of lyrical prose, often spoken through Quatermain: "What is there in the world so desolate as to stand in the streets of a great city and listen to the footsteps falling, falling multitudinous as the rain, and watch the white line of faces as they hurry past, you know not whence, you know not whither? They come and go, their eyes meet yours with a cold stare, for a moment their features are written on your mind, and then they are gone for ever," says Allan in "A Tale of Three Lions." Or Allan remembering his courtship of his wife Stella: "Often I wonder if indeed there are women as sweet as she. Was it solitude that had given such depth and gentleness? Was it the long years of communing with nature that had endowed her with such peculiar grace, the grace we find in opening trees and budding flowers? Had she caught that murmuring voice from the sound of the streams which fall continually about her rocky home? Was it the tenderness of the evening sky beneath which she loved to walk, that lay like a shadow on her face, and the light of the evening stars in her eyes? At the least to me she was the realization of the dream which haunts the sleep of sin-stained men; so my memory paints her, so I hope to find her when at last the sleep has rolled away and the fevered dreams are done."

A pulp writer he was, though, in all senses of the term—as maker of prose in a new genre that wedded "the vulgar but lively influences of the penny dreadfuls, boys' papers, and dime novels with the more literary traditions of the High Victorian novel, creating a vigorous new middlebrow synthesis," as the critic David Pringle says, and as a writer whose books generally appeared first in serial form in actual pulp-paper magazines like *The Popular Magazine, The New Story, Cavalier, Blue Book, Tit-Bits, Adventure, Hutchinson's Story Magazine,* and *The Graphic,* among many others. What Pringle cheerfully calls British "gaslight" writing began about 1883 (when Stevenson's *Treasure Island* appeared in book form, after first being serialized in *Young Folks' Magazine*), and died with everything else Victorian and Edwardian in the First World War. It was a genre led by five towering figures, four of whom remain well known: Stevenson, Kipling, Arthur Conan Doyle, and H. G. Wells. The fifth, who was for much of that time the most popular and best-selling of them all, whose career spanned the whole era, who today is largely obscured even by such one-hit contemporaries of the time as Bram Stoker and Owen Wister, was Rider Haggard.

\* \* \*

*King Solomon's Mines,* to my mind the best of Haggard's books, brings Allan together with two other English adventurers, Sir Henry Curtis (of Brayley Hall, Yorkshire) and Captain John Good (recently of Her Majesty's Navy). Together these three and the stalwart Zulu warrior Ignosi, with a Boer scout and various servants, set off into the vast African wilderness in search of the fabled diamond mines of the biblical King Solomon. After many adventures, a bloodbath of a civil war, and a lovingly detailed fight between Sir Henry and a native king that ends with an axe blow so vicious that the king's head "seemed to spring from his shoulders" and go "rolling and bounding along the ground," our heroes find the treasure, narrowly survive a witch's treachery, and return in triumph to England, Allan having carefully scooped up a fortune. ("If it had not, from the habits of a lifetime, become a sort of second nature with me never to leave anything worth having behind if there was the slightest chance of me being able to carry it away, I am sure I should not have bothered to fill my pockets," he notes.) The book ends cheerfully, with Allan headed to England to see his beloved son Harry and to spend some months with his friends, writing up their incredible adventures.

*Allan Quatermain,* on the other hand, opens darkly: "A week had passed since the funeral of my poor boy Harry, and one evening I was in my room walking up and down and thinking, when there was a ring at the outer door." In walk Sir Henry and Captain Good, and soon enough all three are off again to Africa, this time in search of a mysterious white race said to live deep in the remote wilderness. Again there are many adventures, again "slaughters grim and great" described with unusual verve and attention to gory detail, but this time they are accompanied by the colorful Umslopogaas, and they find not diamonds but an entire civilization, the Zu-Vendi, the Yellow People, so called in part because gold flows like water in their remote land. Haggard here has a wonderful time inventing religious and social mores, and commenting on cultural and linguistic matters, and learnedly discussing architectural and economic theories, but the politics of love and power buck and rear, and the climax of the book is another slaughter in which Umslopogaas dies heroically and Allan sustains the wound that will kill him in the final pages.

"Now I take up my pen for the last time, for I know that the end is at hand," he writes. "All fear of that end has departed, and I feel only as though I were going to sink into the arms of an unutterable rest . . . twenty-four hours more and the world will be gone from me, and with it all its hopes and all its fears . . . 'as the breath of an oxen in winter, as the quick star that runs along the sky, as a little shadow that loses itself at sunset,' as I once heard a Zulu called Ignosi put it, such is the order of our life, the order that passeth away. . . . I am glad to have lived, glad to have known the dear breath of a woman's love, and that true friendship that can even surpass the love of woman; glad to have heard the laughter of little children . . . to have felt the kiss of the salt sea on my face, and watched the wild game trek down to the water in the moonlight. . . . So to all who have known me, or who can think one kindly thought of the old hunter, I stretch out my hand from the far-off shore and bid farewell."

Those were his last written words, reports Sir Henry soberly. The hunter Allan Quatermain died the next morning, at ten minutes after dawn, after one last quiet joke at Captain Good's expense. He died at the same moment his wife Stella had died many years before.

"So passed away a character that I consider went as near perfection as any it has ever been my lot to encounter," writes Sir Henry. "A most intrepid spirit . . . tender, constant, humorous, and possessing many of the qualities that go to make a poet, he was yet almost unrivalled as a man of action and a citizen of the world."

\* \* \*

Rider Haggard went on to a long and successful career after Allan Quatermain's death in 1887 (which occasioned a note to Haggard from, among thousands of other readers, a thirteen-year-old boy who liked *Allan Quatermain* more than *King Solomon's Mines,* as "it is more amusing . . . I hope you will write a great many more books," wrote young Winston Churchill). By 1888 he was easily the best-paid novelist in England (although he was fond of throwing money away on risky mining schemes around the world) and his books were among the first turned into films when the movies slouched into being. Despite regular accusations of plagiarism he was generally lauded by critics and beloved by the reading public; among those who considered him one of the finest writers in the world were Matthew Arnold, Robert Louis Stevenson (whose closest friend in Samoa, where he lived his last five years, was Haggard's brother Bazett), and Rudyard Kipling, who lauded Haggard's "undefeated and joyous imagination" and said of his friend, "I took to him at once, he being the stamp adored by children and trusted by men at sight; and he could tell tales, mainly about himself, that broke up the table."

As the years passed Haggard delved into nonfiction, writing two popular books of rural life, *A Farmer's Year* and *A Gardener's Year,* and a thorough analysis of rural poverty and the nation's maddening land-laws, *Rural England,* for which he visited twenty-six counties at length. He became a vehement advocate for the rural poor against his own land-owning class: A man, he said in a speech in Canada, "looks at the dull masses of misery that pervade the globe, he looks and wonders, and he thinks: is there nothing that I can do to alleviate that misery, to lift up those who are fallen, for their own good and the good of the world? And then he knows that *that,* not the gaudy, exciting work [of writing novels] is the real inspiration of his life."

He grew orchids. He bicycled. He traveled: Egypt, Iceland, New York (where he was interviewed at length by *The New York Times*), New Orleans, Mexico, Cyprus, Italy, the Holy Land, Australia, New Zealand, even Utah, where he admired busy Mormon holdings with a professional farmer's eye. He ran for Parliament, advocating, among other ideas, the banning of all beer taxes and the imposition of a tax on newspapermen who earned more than novelists. (He lost by 198 votes.) He kept a prescient eye on politics, predicting the rise of American power ("sovereignty of the world must ultimately pass to America, with her enormous wealth and natural resources, and

perhaps it is as well that this should be so, as America is our child")
and Germany's resurrection after the First World War ("the
Germans will never forgive nor forget . . . they will live and die to
smash England . . . they will strike her through the heart one day").

He served as a Justice of the Peace, he served as literary editor of
*The African Review* and as president of the Anglo-African Writers'
Club, he worked tirelessly and without pay for twenty years on
governmental and social service committees and boards and com-
missions, including a stint as chairman of the Belgian Agricultural
Restoration Committee in 1915. He became an expert on coastal
erosion in England and Ireland. He befriended Theodore Roosevelt,
William Butler Yeats, Thomas Hardy. He had a knighthood con-
ferred upon him in 1911 and Haggard Glacier and Sir Rider
Mountain named for him in British Columbia.

Yet ever after the first two Allan books there is a continuous
melancholic strain in Haggard, and a startling decline in the energy
and verve of his fiction. His personal losses were considerable: his
mother, with whom he was wonderfully close, died in his arms in
1889; his beloved only son Jock died in 1891, aged nine, of sudden
peritonitis; Haggard and his wife Louisa were more partners than
lovers; his extended family, especially his reckless brothers, sucked
money from him by the barrel; the Boer War washed bloodily over
his beloved southern Africa in 1899; the First World War washed
over his beloved England and Europe in 1914; and he continually
mourned his great love, Lilly Jackson, who died horribly in 1909 of
syphilis acquired from the man she'd married instead of Haggard.
(Haggard quietly paid for her funeral and gravestone.)

He continued to write, so prodigiously as to intimate graphoma-
nia: adventures, often mystical, set in Istanbul, Iceland, Mexico,
Egypt, and Africa; books on farming and history; stories galore; articles of all sorts; lengthy committee reports and papers; thousands of
letters, and an autobiography, published a year after his death, in
which he laid out his theory of dashing writing: "The method of
romance-writing should, in my judgment, be swift, clear, and direct,
with as little padding and as few trappings as possible. The story is
the thing, and every word in the book should be a brick to build its
edifice. Above all, no obscurity should be allowed. Let the characters
be definite, even at the cost of a little crudeness, and so with the
meaning of each sentence. Tricks of 'style' and dark allusions may
please the superior critic; they do not please the average reader . . .
a book is written that it might be read. The first duty of a story is to

keep him who peruses it awake. . . . Such work should be written rapidly and, if possible, not rewritten, since wine of this character loses its bouquet when it is poured from glass to glass. . . . So it comes to this: the way to write a good romance is to sit down and write it almost without stopping."

But what had worked so beautifully for Haggard in 1885 and 1886 worked fitfully the rest of his career. He wrote more than sixty books after *Allan Quatermain*, but even the most rabid Haggard fan would be hard put to say that many of them were very good books. Sydney Higgins, who edited Haggard's diaries for publication in 1980, thinks that Haggard's artistic decline began with his mother's death in 1889 and was cemented by Jock's sudden death two years later, when Haggard and Louisa were vacationing in Mexico. I think maybe it was also the loss of the character he loved best, the character who was the young Haggard, the character who was the wild free Africa he'd known: Allan Quatermain. Few of the later Allan stories have the same zest and humor of the first ones; it's almost as if Allan's fictional death in 1885 was real for Haggard, and filling in the dead man's back story was more labor than pleasure. "Oh, I grow weary of story-telling," he wrote in 1915.

Whatever the cause of his stalled engine—lost love? depression? the fading of Africa in his heart? the loss of his mother as unconscious muse?—it is interesting to note that after 1889 Haggard began to spend most of his time gardening and farming, his mother's two great loves. He took whole years off from writing, he was late on nearly every book and project he agreed to write, and he wrote haltingly when he wrote at all. Whatever it was that had driven him to create Allan and saunter with him through the African veldt, through ferocious battles, into unknown lands, with dear and trusted companions black and white, it was gone.

In the fall of 1924 Haggard was seized with the first of a series of interior pains that were variously diagnosed as gout and infections of the bladder; perhaps they were cancers. His last public appearance was a speech about imagination in literature, in November, after which he retired to his bed in Norfolk and could not muster the energy even to keep his diary, a habit of forty years. By spring his condition was such that his doctors advised an operation in London.

On May 9 he rose early and was dressed by his nurse. As he sat exhausted in his chair he "looked down at his overcoat as if something was missing, then got up, walked to the table where there was a bowl of daffodils, and taking one out pulled it through his button-hole," wrote his daughter Lilias later.

This gesture broke his wife's heart; Haggard went nowhere without a flower in his lapel, a rose or carnation in summer, an orchid in winter.

"Rider, do you really want to go, dear?" asked his wife Louie. "You have only got to say if you don't and we will send the ambulance back—are you quite, quite sure?"

But off he went, "to the operation he guessed would be final," wrote Graham Greene (whose favorite book was *King Solomon's Mines*). The operation was "entirely successful," according to his doctors, but for the next three days Haggard lay silently before fading into a coma. He died on the morning of May 14.

"The dawn came, the sun rose in the east," wrote Allan Quatermain of his beloved wife's last minutes. "His rays were reflected in glory upon the bosom of the western sky . . . she fixed her dying eyes on the splendour of the morning sky. She looked on me and smiled as an angel might smile. Then with a last effort she lifted her hand, and, pointing to the radiant heavens, whispered: *There, Allan, there!*"

CHAPTER SIX

# How Many of You Are There in the Quartet?

The late saxophone player Paul Desmond, whose martini-dry sound was the engine behind the Dave Brubeck Quartet, was reportedly working on a memoir up until he died in 1977. He never finished it. There are a number of theories as to why he never finished it. One story is that he would tear it up and start over whenever he got close to a finished manuscript. Another story is that he talked about it but never actually wrote any of it—a tale belied by the appearance, in 1973, of an ostensible chapter of the book in *Punch*. A third story is that he wrote only when he was not sipping Scotch, and so never wrote much.

Desmond himself liked to talk about the book, although he conceded to a reporter, "It's largely a fraud. That's my cover story. I had thought of writing a book before I began hanging out at Elaine's, and found that most of the heavy writers there had Walter Mitty dreams about being jazz players."

But this cover story that he didn't really work on the book was itself a cover story, because perhaps he did work on it a good deal without telling anyone, says his friend Dave Brubeck. Or maybe he wrote some and then scrapped the results, suggests his friend Iola Brubeck, Dave's wife. Or maybe he didn't write it at all, says his friend Gene Lees, because you could never be sure of anything with Paul, a man of smiles and shadows and illusions who was just as adept at telling stories that might or might not be true as he was at playing the alto saxophone.

\* \* \*

For example, his name wasn't Paul Desmond; it was Paul Breitenfeld. He was born in San Francisco in 1924, son of a man who played the organ in silent movies and of a mother whose emotional problems occasioned her son being sent to live with cousins in New York for six years. As a boy Paul picked up the violin, which his father detested and forbade him to play (a stricture for which Desmond later thanked his father in the liner notes on one of his records). At age twelve, while a student at San Francisco Polytechnic High, he picked up the clarinet. At eighteen, as a freshman at San Francisco State College, he picked up the alto saxophone—perhaps, suggests Brubeck, simply because he liked the clean sweet sound.

That same year he joined the Army and was assigned to the 253rd Army Band, in which he spent the next three years. "A great way to spend the war," he recalled. "We expected to get shipped out every month, but it never happened. Somewhere in Washington our file must still be on the floor under a desk."

One day early in 1944 there were auditions for soldiers desperate to get in the band. One of these young soldiers was a rifleman named David Brubeck, son of a rancher and rodeo roper from deep in the California outback. The sax player Dave Van Kriedt, already in the Army band, remembers that Brubeck played superbly in the audition, but that the rest of the band wasn't all that impressed. Brubeck remembers nervously starting a blues in B flat with his left hand and in G with his right hand (a trick called polytonality) to see what the sax player would do. Desmond, on sax, remembered thinking the pianist was "stark raving mad," but he also remembered adjusting easily, jamming briskly through a set of tunes, and saying to Brubeck afterward, "Man, like wigsville—you really grooved me with those nutty changes," to which Brubeck replied (according to Desmond, never a fully reliable source), "White man speak with forked tongue." It's worth noting that Desmond told this story only after Brubeck told him that there was reputedly Cherokee blood in the Brubeck family line.

Brubeck made the band, although he did end up being shipped overseas in 1944, "touring in a band with the Rockettes," according to Desmond, and then ending up with Patton's Third Army near Verdun, France, during the Battle of the Bulge. His unit was headed to the front when a visiting USO band with a sick pianist called for a piano player from the audience. Brubeck volunteered, and so impressed a colonel that he was held back from the front and made the centerpiece of a new band, the Wolf Pack—the first integrated band in the United States Army. This band once got lost on its way to a gig and ended up in German territory; Brubeck, the driver, spun the truck around and raced back to the Allied lines, where an American guard held two live grenades with the pins pulled over Brubeck's lap until he was convinced they were really American soldiers. Brubeck remembers that there was dynamite hung from the trees by the guard post and that the guard told him he had just lost friends to Germans who drove up to the post in an American truck with American uniforms. He also says he still has nightmares regularly about that moment in Germany, nearly sixty years later.

* * *

Desmond once told the pianist Marian McPartland that he had been stunned by Brubeck's bizarre chord changes and time experiments during the 1944 audition, and that he and Brubeck had hit it off immediately without a word being exchanged. If so, their mutual regard was challenged as soon as the war ended. Brubeck got a job leading a trio called the Three Ds at the Geary Cellar in San Francisco (one of the Ds being the muscular sax player Darryl Cutler, who liked to wear heavy makeup, later taught hand-to-hand combat to military recruits, and served as the bar's ferocious bouncer, throwing rowdy patrons up the stairs into the street). Desmond got a job leading a combo at the Bandbox in Palo Alto. Desmond sat in a few nights with Brubeck at the Geary, and then hired away the whole band, keeping Brubeck on piano but cutting his pay from $100 a week to $42.

Nearly as bad as the pay was the song the band was required to sing every night—a song written by Desmond for the occasion:

It's the Bandbox
That's the joint for you
The whiskey is old
But the music is new
At the Bandbox
Where the proletariat
Make merry

Soon, for Brubeck, matters bottomed out altogether, for Desmond first took the band to a new job at the remote Feather River Inn (from which he could easily reach Reno to gamble) and then hired a new piano player, leaving Brubeck, now married with two children, unemployed. Brubeck found a job after a few weeks at a dingy bar in Clear Lake, deep in the country, and then slowly worked his way back to the coast as the leader of a trio—piano, bass, drums. By 1951 his trio, now ensconced at the Blackhawk in San Francisco after two years at the Burma Lounge in Oakland, was locally famous and performing weekly on Jimmy Lyons' KNBC radio show, "The Lyons Den," which could be heard from Seattle to San Diego—and far out to sea, which explained the large numbers of sailors and merchant mariners who crammed the Blackhawk when their ships were in.

Desmond, who had gone to New York City in 1950 to play with Jack Fina's band (with which he often played clarinet), heard a Brubeck trio recording one night on the radio and immediately headed west again, dead-set on joining the very pianist he'd let go at the Feather River Inn. "He wanted to be in the band so badly," remembered the quartet's original bassist, Ron Crotty. "He made no secret about it. He used to say, 'I'm going to be playing with Brubeck. He's my piano player. I'm going to be in that band.'"

One day Desmond appeared on Brubeck's doorstep in San Francisco, and Iola let him in, despite strict prohibitions from her husband against exactly such a catastrophe, while Dave was out back hanging diapers out to dry. Dave and Iola had three small children by then and there were a lot of diapers.

Why did she let him in?

"He was so charming, and so forlorn," she says. "I walked him through our flat out to the back porch, where Dave was hanging laundry."

Desmond "groveled," by his own account, offering to wash the car.

No, said Brubeck.

I'll play for half-wages, said Desmond.

No.

I'll play for nothing.

No.

I'll . . . *babysit*, said Desmond.

Okay, said Brubeck.

They then signed a most unusual contract, by which Brubeck agreed to never fire Desmond, to act in all capacities as leader of the quartet, and to give Desmond twenty percent of all profits. So began the Dave Brubeck Quartet, which soon was on the road for three hundred performances a year, from sea to shining sea, and eventually abroad as far as India and the Middle East. From its inception in 1951 until its demise on the evening of December 26, 1967, the group released some forty records, among them the immensely popular *Jazz Goes to College* (and its sequels *Jazz Goes to Junior College* and *Jazz Goes to High School*) and the jazz classic *Time Out*. In a 1961 profile of the group, The New Yorker called the Quartet "the world's best-paid, most widely traveled, most highly publicized, and most popular small group now playing improvised syncopated music."

\* \* \*

The first jazz song to sell a million copies was "Take Five," a song performed by the Dave Brubeck Quartet and written by Paul Desmond, in 1959. The song was on *Time Out*, and was explained away by Desmond as a song that allowed him a cigarette break during performances. "Take Five," said Desmond, "was never supposed to be a hit. It was supposed to be a Joe Morello drum solo"—solos so famously long and loud that Desmond was in the habit of retreating backstage to read during the barrage. On other occasions Desmond would say that the 5/4 time signature came to him while he was playing a slot machine ("pull-spin-spin, click-click," wrote the critic Will Thornbury).

"All nonsense," says Brubeck, laughing. "The song began as a beat that Joe used to warm up before shows. Paul would loosen up sometimes by improvising over Joe. I finally told Paul to put a melodic line on the thing and he came back with two themes and the complaint that he just couldn't write anything in 5/4 time. But the two themes were excellent, so I suggested that we open with one, use the second as a bridge, and then come home again—AABA, you know. Which worked. I suggested that we call it 'Take Five,' for the odd time and for the idea that it was a drummer's break in the set. Paul hated the title, but it stuck."

Desmond the composer was as elusive an entity as Desmond the player or the author, unlike Brubeck, who had wanted to be a composer all along, composed constantly, dreamed of spending most of his year composing classical music, and still composes daily between dawn and breakfast. Desmond composed fitfully and beautifully, the same way he wrote prose. "He was an occasional composer, that's probably the best way to say it," says Doug Ramsey. "And most of his tunes are based on the harmonic structures of other tunes, which is common among jazz 'composers.' You play a song for a while and it gets into your head and for fun you fiddle with it and take it somewhere else. His song 'Wendy,' for example, is based on the song 'For All We Know,' and his bossa nova songs are mostly based on other tunes. He was also a composer of necessity—very good at impromptu creative composition when it suddenly came time for a recording date."

Fitful and occasional and prompted by necessity his composing may have been, but he quietly piled up a body of work: in all he wrote twenty-seven songs alone, seven more with Dave Brubeck, one with Iola Brubeck (a vocal version of the instrumental "Take Five"), and one, sort of, with the blind English pianist George Shearing—a jazz arrangement of the Christmas song "God Rest Ye Merry Gentlemen."

Today the Desmond Music Company of New York City processes all performance and recording matters for Desmond's work in the United States, and the Derry Music Company of San Rafael (established by Dave Brubeck) handles all Desmond matters outside the United States. By far the most-requested of Desmond's songs around the world is "Take Five," which is certainly the most popular and remunerative cigarette break in history.

* * *

There are endless stories of Desmond jokes, puns, dry witticisms. The most famous Desmond line was "I think I had it in the back of my mind that I wanted to sound like a dry martini," which haunted him the rest of his career and appeared in nearly every account of him and his music. But there were many others. After a woman left him for a Wall Street broker, he remarked that "the world ends not with a whim but a banker." After noticing a newspaper photograph of Aristotle Onassis in front of Buster Keaton's house in Hollywood, he said to Iola Brubeck, "Hmm—Aristotle contemplating the home of Buster." He and guitarist Jim Hall were always planning a *Jazz Goes to Ireland* record on which would be songs like "Fitzhugh or No One." Among his compositions are the "Battle Hymn of the Republican" and "Sacre Blues." He claimed to be the world's slowest alto player and to have received prestigious awards for his slowness. He claimed that practice made him play too fast. He called himself the John P. Marquand of the alto sax. He claimed that he had picked the name Desmond at random from the telephone directory and that he didn't like his given name, Breitenfeld, because it sounded "too Irish." He said that the only reason he was in the Quartet was to be able to lean on Brubeck's piano during a show, which drove Brubeck crazy. He said that he liked playing with the guitarist Jim Hall because he liked to try to lean on the guitar during shows, which drove Hall crazy. To an interviewer he once said that "You're beginning to sound like a cross between David Frost and David Susskind, and that is a cross I cannot bear." His friend Doug Ramsey remembers being on a crowded elevator with him once when a bell rang. "What's that?" asked a startled passenger. "E-flat," they said simultaneously, which started a friendship that lasted twenty years.

The same adjectives used to describe his talk—witty, humorous, dry—surface when people try to describe the way in which he played the alto saxophone. It's essentially impossible to accurately describe the tone and style of an instrument being played masterfully, but every jazz writer and many fellow musicians tried with Desmond and his horn: "Profoundly beautiful and lyrical," said the alto saxophonist Julian Adderley, better known as the Cannonball. "Wonderful and lyrical," said the alto saxophonist Jackie McLean. "Exceptionally light in texture and pure in tone, casually luxurious, cerebral, and exquisitely lyrical," said the critic Leonard Feather. "Insouciant and lyrical," said the critic Whitney Baillet. "Disciplined, brilliant, and lyrical," says the critic Gene Lees. "Extremely economical, very cool, quite melodic, and lyrical," says the scholar Mark Gridley. "Melodic, organized, and lyrical," says the scholar Ted Gioia. "Simple, swinging, and lyrical," says the drummer Joe Dodge, who first played with Desmond in a dance band before they were in the early Quartet together. "Pure, ingenious, resourceful, witty, literate, sophisticated, personal, appealing, and lyrical," said the critic Doug Ramsey, a dear friend. "Gentle and lyrical," says Noel Silverman, another friend. "The greatest lyrical player there's ever been," says Dave Brubeck.

Or here's a simple description: "My favorite alto player in the world," said the late Charlie Parker.

\* \* \*

"The years have been crammed with more than enough things— funny and otherwise—to fill a fair-sized book, which, if you can hang about for another year or so, I will have finished," wrote Desmond in 1976. The book was to be titled *How Many of You Are There in the Quartet?*, a question he claimed he was asked every day by fans and airline stewardesses.

His friends mostly thought he was for real. "He talked a lot about the book he was working on, a book of his memoirs," said Bob Prince, the arranger and conductor who worked with Desmond on the 1961 and 1962 sessions later released as *Late Lament*. Jim Hall thought he was working on it, although Hall also remembers Desmond telling Gerry Mulligan that the book would never be finished, and that when his executors opened his trunk they would find not a pile of unpublished manuscripts but empty milk cartons.

What might Desmond's memoir have contained? Certainly more stories of the Quartet, which in its heyday traveled the world, even unto India where drummer Joe Morello, from the working-class mill town of Springfield, Massachusetts, wowed the local tabla drummers during improvised jazz ragas. Stories of the dance bands he played in before the Quartet, of the endless trios and quartets and quintets he formed and dissolved and reformed to get club dates when he was in his hungry twenties in San Francisco. Stories perhaps of his brief marriage in college, about which he talked to no one; his friend Gene Lees mentioned the subject once, when both men were in their cups, and watched in dismay as Desmond wept silently. Stories of his most extraordinary musical moments, like the roaring hours he remembered with Brubeck in San Francisco in the late 1940s, or the legendary 1952 sessions at Boston's Storyville jazz club, sessions that both Desmond and Brubeck remembered as perhaps their greatest moments as musical partners, or nights at the Feather River Inn when Desmond said he and Brubeck were mind-locked and playing in three keys at once. Stories of how he became close friends with Charlie Parker and Chet Baker, perhaps the most talented horn players and heroin addicts in the history of jazz. Stories of discovering he had lung cancer after going in to the doctor for pain in his foot. Stories of his dear friend the guitarist Jim Hall, with whom he spent nearly as many hours playing and talking as he did with Brubeck. Stories of the Army band in which he and Brubeck met, and how he and Iola met, and how he had a crush on Iola, and how Iola met Dave, working on a college radio show together, the Friday Frolics at the University of the Pacific, where Dave played piano and Iola did comedy sketches. Stories of Paul's college days, during which he desperately wanted to be a writer. Stories of the thousands of hours he must have practiced on his horn, although he claimed he never practiced because it made him play too fast. Stories of his years living with his cousins in New York. Stories of meeting the alto player Art Pepper, who was also, eerily, a

California boy farmed out to relatives at age five and enamored first of the clarinet. Stories of his first memories of music, in kindergarten, when he was given bells to play, and during a show for the parents played not what he was supposed to but his own impromptu composition, which wowed the crowd and perhaps sent him toward jazz. Stories of his mother's troubles. Stories of his stern father who played the organ in movie theaters as silent movies flickered across the huge screen. Stories of his kind father meeting Brubeck on Market Street in San Francisco and begging Brubeck to keep Paul in the band when Paul's unruly habits were driving Brubeck crazy. Stories of the first moments when jazz flickered into his ears, when his mind startled awake to rhythm and melody and harmony and scales and chords and picked out a soloing clarinet line, the horn player slipping in and out and away and through and between and above the bars of the tune with a supple playful gentle grace that was somehow symmetrical and organized yet altogether free and exuberant and joyous all at once.

I remember when jazz sneaked into me: late on a summer afternoon in New York, when I was thirteen. My sister took me into a little jazz club. It was dark inside, velvety dark. We sat in the corner. My sister ordered coffee. There was a quartet. Their instruments glinted and glittered in the soft dark. There was no singer, which meant that the music flowed on its own, one song into another, no words, no language but the liquid ladders of the chord changes. I remember there was a saxophone and a trumpet and they took turns mewling muttering moaning groaning growling barking brassing shouting singing shimmering into the dusky room. Waiters and customers passed our table, darker vertical lines against the general charcoal of the air. Glasses shone on the bar, a brass railing glimmered. My sister didn't say much and I said nothing and after an hour or so we emerged blinking from the bar like fish rising from rich dark water, and I was never afterwards the same man.

### *Interlude*

In March of 1954, WHDH radio listeners in the greater Boston area were treated to an interview of the sax player Charlie Parker by the sax player Paul Desmond. Both men were in Boston to play club dates, Parker at the High Hat and Desmond with the Quartet at Storyville. No one is quite sure how Desmond came to be interviewing Bird the year before that talented and troubled genius died at thirty-five, or how the two came to be good friends, but the transcript of the interview is a sort of poem. Some excerpts:

Desmond: *Did you realize the effect you were going to have on jazz—that you were going to change the entire scene?*

Parker: Well, let's put it like this—no.

*What do you want from your music?*

I've thought it should be very clean, very precise—as clean as possible, you know. And more or less to the people, you know. Something that's beautiful, you know. There's definitely stories and stories and stories that can be told in the musical idiom, you know. Music is basically melody, harmony, and rhythm, but people can do much more with music than that. It can be very descriptive in all kinds of ways, you know, all walks of life. Don't you agree, Paul?

*Yep. Where'd you get your fantastic technique?*

I can't see where there's anything fantastic about it all. I put quite a bit of study into the horn. The neighbors asked my mother to move when we were living out West [in Kansas City, Missouri]. I was driving them crazy with the horn. I put in fifteen hours a day for four years.

*That's very reassuring to hear, because somehow I got the idea that you were just sort of born with it.*

Study is absolutely necessary, in all forms. Schooling is one of the most wonderful things there's ever been, you know.

*Where did you first meet Dizzy Gillespie?*

On the bandstand of the Savoy Ballroom in New York City in 1939. I was quite fascinated with the fellow, and we became very good friends. That was the first time I ever had the pleasure to meet Dizzy Gillespie.

*Was he playing the same way then?*

He was playing what you might call a beaucoup of horn.

*Beaucoup horn?*

Yes.

*Okay.*

You know, just like all the horn packed up at once, you know.

*Right. How far I was behind all this.*

Don't be that way, Paul. Modesty will get you nowhere.

*New York was jumping in 1942, was it not?*

New York was. Those were the good old days, you know, Paul? Gay youth, lack of funds. There was nothing to do but play, you know, and we had a lot of fun trying to play, you know. I did plenty of jam sessions, much late hours, plenty of good food, nice clean living, you know. But basically speaking—much poverty.

*That's always good—no worries.*

But now I have the pleasure to work with other young fellows, you know, that come along. Fellows like you, yourself, Paul.

*Thank you.*

I'd like to study some more. I'm going to try to go to Europe to study. I had the pleasure to meet one Edgar Varèse recently. He's a classical composer from France, very nice fellow, and he wants to teach me. I might have the chance to go to the Academy of Music in Paris and study, you know. My prime interest still is learning to play music, you know.

*How did you meet Miles Davis?*

I met Miles in 1944, in St. Louis, when he was a youngster

and was still going to school. This was when Billy Eckstine had formed his own organization. Dizzy was in that band, and a lot of other fellows, and last and least, yours truly.

*Modesty will get you nowhere, Charlie.*

## Solo

Dave Brubeck broke up the Dave Brubeck Quartet on the day after Christmas in 1967. He had given everyone a year's notice but no one believed him until the very last set. The band played in a hotel ballroom in Pittsburgh and then retreated upstairs and had a terrific party complete with a box of apples sent up by the musician Paul Winter and his mother.

It was an amicable parting, as such things go: Brubeck wanted to compose and be with his family, all four of the members were tired of the ferocious schedule, and all four were still friends, even after many thousands of miles and performances and car rides and planes and buses and sticky summer mornings in small towns with bad food and no toothbrush and a sound system borrowed from the high school audio-visual department.

In the years after the Quartet closed up shop, Brubeck kept playing and recording—often with his sons Darius, Chris, and Danny, with whom he often toured. Gene Wright, who had formed his own big band, the Dukes of Swing, in Chicago when he was twenty years old, kept playing—forming new bands, recording with Tony Bennett, doing television and movie music in Los Angeles, and finally becoming chairman of the Jazz Department at the University of Cincinnati. Joe Morello, who had played with Marian McPartland and Stan Kenton before joining the Quartet in 1956, kept playing, recording a little, writing books about drumming, teaching drumming.

Paul Desmond, who had played the sax every night for a quarter of a century, apparently stopped cold. He took up residence in an apartment on 55th Street in New York City and by some accounts did not even touch his horn for three years. Brubeck wonders if he even opened the instrument's case.

He worked on his book, maybe. He sipped Scotch. He certainly read; Brubeck has said that Desmond might well have been the most literary-minded jazzman in history. His friend Doug Ramsey says Desmond never went anywhere without a paperback in his pocket, and that Walker Percy was among his favorite writers. His friend

Noel Silverman remembers that Desmond always read fiction and that Edna O'Brien was among his favorite writers. He tinkered with electronic gadgets; he was fascinated with the most modern sound technology and machinery of all sorts. He talked on the phone for hours, remembers Ramsey. He talked, he hung out. He went out at night, to Elaine's, Bradley's, Reno Sweeney's, and often to the Half Note, which he liked, he said, because it was so close to his apartment. He ate daily at the French Shack, a restaurant he liked, he said, because it was so close to his apartment. He "conducted his intricate and mysterious romantic entanglements, which even he didn't understand," says Ramsey carefully. (It is interesting to note that a number of his songs are women's names: Audrey, Mili, Susie, Wendy.) He went to hear musicians he admired: Zoot Sims, Al Cohn, Blossom Dearie, Lee Konitz, Bill Evans. Many times the musicians he admired, who admired him, asked him to sit in with their shows, and he would gently decline—even though, as Doug Ramsey notes, Desmond loved to play "anything, with anyone, at a moment's notice."

Money was no particular worry, what with royalties from his songs and recordings. He entertained offers for his book, and met with publishers and agents here and there, but no contracts were signed. He played the piano some—his friend Don Thompson says Desmond could play a sharp piano, and the one he had in his apartment was reputed to be the best in New York City.

But how he filled his days no one knows, not even Brubeck. Perhaps they were dark days. "There's an area in Paul that he hasn't been able to realize yet," said the alto sax player Lee Konitz in 1960. "That's why he gets so depressed—he needs more time to know himself, so that he will get to like himself better. I don't think he has enough time for reflection and thought. I feel that Paul has experienced greatness, and once this feeling of playing what you really hear has been felt by a player, it's difficult to settle for less than this."

"If you knew the story, you could forgive Paul anything," Brubeck has famously and mysteriously remarked about his friend—a remark he has never elucidated, and never will, he says. "A deeply private man," says Iola Brubeck. "Charming and funny, and he had many friends, but he departmentalized or compartmentalized his friends, in a sense—he had drinking friends, musical friends, literary friends, romantic friends, and the circles rarely if ever overlapped."

"He was the loneliest man I ever met," says his friend Gene Lees. "Astonishingly selfish, in that he was totally focused on himself, not one to give of his inner feelings, although he was very generous and not at all greedy. He just did what he did and that was his focus. I adored the man. He was brilliant beyond belief in person and as a musician, and extraordinarily fun to be around, and very alone. I don't know what he did with his days. No one knows, not even Dave. There'll probably never be a biography of Paul. Jazz musicians don't lead interesting lives. They're not tragic operas, except for the occasional Charlie Parker or Billie Holiday. They mostly just play the hell out of their instruments and then go home and practice."

### Chorus

In 1971 Desmond was coaxed out of retirement by Jim Hall, who persuaded him to play some quartet dates at the Half Note in New York City. Desmond claimed he only took the job because the Half Note was around the corner and he could roll out of bed to work. His shows crammed the club. He played with Gerry Mulligan at the New Orleans Jazz Festival, a performance that drew a roaring crowd and ecstatic reviews from critics. He played a Christmas concert in New York's Town Hall that year with the Modern Jazz Quartet, which drew a roaring crowd and finished with "Take Five."

In 1972 Chet Baker persuaded him into the studio for two albums and Brubeck persuaded him back on stage for a series of concerts called "Two Generations of Brubeck," which featured Brubeck sons Chris, Danny, and Darius. Jim Hall then persuaded him to meet the Canadian jazz guitarist Ed Bickert in Toronto, and Bickert and Desmond played so well together that Desmond played a series of club dates in Toronto, made a studio record, taped a series of live performances, appeared on a Canadian television show, and played the Edmonton Jazz Festival with his Canadian quartet—billed as the Paul Desmond Quartet, the first such entity since Desmond's scuffling years in San Francisco after the war.

Finally, in 1976, Brubeck persuaded Desmond back into the Brubeck Quartet for a wildly popular (and characteristically busy) Silver Anniversary Tour—twenty-five shows in twenty-five nights in twenty-five cities. They opened in Alfred, New York, and then played twenty-three shows in twenty-three nights, traveling from one gig to the next on a bus with eight beds, two television sets, a kitchen, two bathrooms, a shower, and two audio recording systems. The plan was to record the last three shows, and from these issue a record.

Joe Morello, who'd had problems with his eyes since he was a child, had detached a retina just before the reunion tour and lost sight in one eye. His doctor told him to go ahead and make the tour, with one proviso; that if he noticed any change in the other eye, he was to return to Boston immediately for surgery.

During the first set of the twenty-third show, in Fort Wayne, Indiana, as Brubeck took a solo, Morello asked Wright if there was a green spotlight on them.

No, said Wright.

Is the auditorium lit in green? asked Morello.

No, said Wright.

When the set ended Morello and Brubeck huddled in the corner of the stage, where Morello reported that his world had gone darker and darker green until it had finally faded altogether soon after the song "Don't Worry 'bout Me." He could not see at all. "Bru, I can't even see you right now," he said.

Brubeck's son Danny took over the drumming. That night the Quartet stayed up most of the night talking. In the morning Brubeck promised Morello that they'd plan another tour together if the operation went well and he regained some sight. As the bus passed under Morello's motel room on its way to the penultimate show, Brubeck honked the opening notes of "Blue Rondo" and Morello tore open his curtains. "This huge man in his jockey shorts stood there and waved," says Brubeck. "We knew he couldn't see us. That was the last time we saw Joe for a while."

The Quartet, now with Danny Brubeck on drums, finished the tour and disbanded again. Months later Brubeck released a record of the reunion tour. The last song on the album, featuring Joe Morello on drums, was the version of "Don't Worry 'bout Me" recorded in Fort Wayne before Morello's world faded out.

"I think we all felt those years were worth it, and we were all glad to be back together," says Brubeck. "What I sensed out of the reunion was a great love among four terribly independent individuals. No matter what we put each other through over the years—and believe me, the emotions ran the full gamut—there was deep love and regard there."

## Interlude

The October 1973 number of *Punch*, the venerable British humor magazine, included a brief essay called "How Many of You Are There in the Quartet?," by the American jazz saxophonist Paul Desmond. Excerpts:

"Dawn. A station wagon pulls up to the office of an obscure motel in New Jersey. Three men enter—pasty-faced, grim-eyed, silent (for those are their names). Perfect opening shot, before credits, for a really lousy bank-robbery movie? Wrong. The Dave Brubeck Quartet, some years ago, starting our day's work.

"Today we have a contract for two concerts at the Orange County State Fair in Middletown. 2 p.m. and 8 p.m. Brubeck likes to get to the job early. So we pull up behind this hay truck around noon, finally locating the guy who had signed the contract. Stout, red-necked, gruff, and harried (from the old New Jersey law firm of the same name), he peers into the station wagon, which contains four musicians, bass, drums, and assorted baggage, and for the first and only time in our seventeen years of wandering around the world, we get this question: 'Where's the piano?'

"Our bandstand is a wooden platform, about ten feet high and immense. Evidently no piano has been located in Orange County, since the only props on stage are a vintage electric organ and one mike. Behind us is a fair-sized tent containing about two hundred people, in which a horse show for young teenagers is currently in progress—sched-uled, we soon discover, to continue throughout our concert. This is hazardous mainly because their sound system is vastly superior to ours.

"So we begin our desperation opener, 'St. Louis Blues.' Brubeck, who has never spent more than ten minutes of his life at an electric organ, much less the one he is now at, is producing sounds like an early synthesizer. (Later he makes a few major breakthroughs, like locating the volume control pedal and figuring out how to wiggle his right hand, achiev-ing a tremolo effect similar to Jimmy Smith with a terminal hangover, but doesn't help much.) Eugene Wright, our noble bass player, and me take turns schlepping the mike back and forth between us and playing grouchy, doomed choruses, but the only sound we can hear comes from our friendly neigh-borhood horse show. 'LOPE,' it roars. 'CANTER ... TROT ... AND THE WINNER IN THE TWELVE-YEAR-OLD CLASS IS

... JACQUELINE HIGGS!'

"As always in difficult situations such as these, we turn to our main man, primo virtuoso of the group, the Maria Callas of the drums, Joe Morello, who has rescued us from disaster from Grand Forks to Rajkot, India.

"'You got it,' we said, 'stretch out,' which ordinarily is like issuing an air travel card to a hijacker. And, to his eternal credit, Morello outdoes himself. All cymbals sizzling, all feet working. Now he's into triplets around the tom-toms, which has shifted foundations from the Odeon Hammersmith to Free Trade Hall and turned Buddy Rich greener than usual with envy.

"The horse show is suddenly silent. Fanning in the stands has subsided slightly. Suddenly a figure emerges from the horse tent, hurtles to the side of the stage, and yells at Brubeck, 'For Chrissakes, could you tell the drummer not to play so loud? He's terrifying the horses.'

"Never a group to accept defeat gracelessly, we play a sort of Muzak for a suitable period and split. Later, four pasty-faced, grim-eyed men pile into a station wagon and drive away. It may not be bank robbery, but it's a living."

After this essay appeared in *Punch*—a chapter of the book, Desmond told everyone—he never published again.


## Coda

In February of 1977 Desmond joined the Quartet on stage at Avery Fisher Hall for a reunion concert, at which he played beautifully, remembers Brubeck, "though he could hardly stand and should never have been out of bed. He'd had transfusions throughout the day just so he could play that night. Two doctors came with him to the show and were amazed he could even stand up. But playing music heals and invigorates you." Brubeck, among others, noticed that Paul had to use two or three breaths for long notes rather than the one great gulp he'd needed in the past.

Sometime after that show, remembers Brubeck, he and Desmond did a recording session of about three hours, just the two of them; the next day they recorded for another hour or so, after which Paul observed that "we can make an album for a streetcar token and a ham sandwich." That was the last time Brubeck saw Desmond, though they spent many hours on the phone and "got closer and closer," says Brubeck.

Desmond made plans to record once more with his Canadian quartet, and he welcomed a string of visitors to his apartment (among them Charles Mingus, dressed in a swirling black cape and cowboy hat). None of the members of the Quartet wanted Paul to be alone, so Joe Morello sent one of his drumming students to live with Desmond. He wrote a will; Noel Silverman, his attorney, remembers asking if Paul wanted to set up a music scholarship at his alma mater, San Francisco State, and Paul replying that no, there were already enough bad saxophone players in the world.

In late May, Desmond called his friend Doug Ramsey in Texas and made a drinking date at Elaine's. Then he died on May 30, alone in his apartment, of lung cancer—with, as he had noted with amusement to Ramsey a few days before, "a pristine, perfect liver, one of the great livers of our time, awash in Dewars and full health." He was fifty-two.

He left his alto saxophone to the Brubecks' son Michael, with whom he was close. He left his piano to his friend Bradley Cunningham, owner of the jazz club Bradley's. He left his wristwatch to his doctor. He made small bequests to a few friends and remote cousins. His walls of books were sold to a dealer; Noel Silverman, his attorney and executor, found no manuscripts among Desmond's papers.

By Paul's instruction there was no funeral or memorial, and his remains were cremated and scattered at Big Sur in California, south of San Francisco. The proceeds from his compositions and from his recordings were sent to the American Red Cross, which now earns more than $100,000 a year from his music. In the twenty-four years since his death, Paul Desmond has given the Red Cross more than three million dollars.

Dave Brubeck, the rodeo roper's son, forged on after Desmond's death, touring, recording, composing ballets, fugues, chorales, symphonies, musicals, oratorios, cantatas, even a Mass. His work is performed all over the world, often by the pianist Dave Brubeck; he and Iola just returned from a tour of Europe, during which Dave played a set every night. He is now eighty years old and says that he composes every day whether sick or well, and plays if he feels well, and if he is sick then he plays until he feels better.

Asked what he was happiest about in his career, his greatest achievement, the highlight of his sixty years as a musician, he says, "I got together with Paul. That was most important of all."

CHAPTER SEVEN

# A Small Note about *Big Red*

Iwas ten years old when I read the "boys' novel" *Big Red* for the first time, in 1966. There was a much-publicized new edition of the book out that year, twenty-one years after its first edition, and five years after a popular Disney movie of the book had taken peculiar license with the plot, unaccountably adding French-Canadian accents and roles. *Big Red* was given to me as a Christmas present by one of my two uncles, a reserved and exclusively urban man who had very probably never set foot in a forest in his life, let alone plumbed the sort of dense woods in which *Big Red* is set: an odd gift from a gentle and mysterious man.

I read *Red* mostly on the floor, sprawled on a golden carpet lit by fat bars of sunlight, and it seems to me I read it mostly on late afternoons, often with snacks in hand and dribbling over pages, for I remember the last light of wintry days bending into the room, and the crunch of cracker-crumbs between pages when the book was ordered closed by my parents herding their progeny to dinner. Three decades later I reread the book, and again digested it while supine, but this time I read it sans crackers and abed late at night, a middle-aged man's time to himself, the day's labors and laughters concluded. Near me now on second read were not ingots of winter light but a wife and three children, all asleep, not a one interested in the sylvan perambulations of seventeen-year-old Danny Pickett and the big red Irish setter that was the love of his life.

The man who created Danny and his dog was a former trapper and surveyor named Jim Kjelgaard. *Big Red* was Kjelgaard's third book for Holiday House, which had asked him to try a boys' book in 1941, after being impressed by his outdoor stories in magazines. Kjelgaard's first two books for Holiday, *Forest Patrol* and *Rebel Siege,* had sold modestly, but *Big Red* took off running—225,000 copies by 1956, the Disney movie of the book in 1961, nearly a million copies sold in its first fifty years—and it is still in print, most recently by

Bantam Books. Red and Danny were so very popular that Kjelgaard wrote about them again in *Irish Red* (1951) and *Outlaw Red* (1953), which nominally star Red's sons Mike and Sean, respectively, but are really about the same subtle subjects that pervade *Big Red:* the mysterious, dangerous, entrancingly remote deep woods of the Allegheny Mountains in the early twentieth century; the wild animals of those woods and the ways that they live and die; Danny's precocious maturity, independence, and knowledge of those woods and their denizens; the behavior, conduct, training, and use of hunting and show dogs; and the many ways in which men and dogs respect and love each other.

James Arthur Kjelgaard wrote forty-six books, all told, before he died in 1959, at age forty-eight. Nearly all his books were for teenagers and about animals, and they are as a rule well written, clear, and suspenseful, but it is *Big Red* that is Kjelgaard's primary literary legacy, and reading through it and its two sequels again after three decades has been an edifying pleasure. I learned many things that I did not notice when I was ten years old and sprawled on the floor gobbling crackers.

I noticed that Kjelgaard tries hard to explain the story as a whole by talking again and again about how breeding dogs for certain skills and appearances is a valorous and virtuous thing (this line of talk explains the presence of Red's owner, the millionaire dog-breeder Mister Haggin, played by the dapper Walter Pidgeon in the Disney movie), but I also noticed that Kjelgaard's heart is in hunting, not bloodlines, and scenes set in New York City at a dog show ring false. They are too civilized, too much set-pieces placed on the stage to illustrate the virtue of dog breeding, and they have none of the muddy excitement of the rest of the books, in which all the action takes place in the woods.

I also noticed that another repeated theme is Danny's speedy maturation. In *Big Red,* Danny comes to love Red intensely and so is brought to the realization that his career will not be running traplines in the deep forest but raising hunting and show dogs; by the end of the book, in which he and Red together battle and defeat a relentless wolverine and a monstrous bear, he has become a thoughtful and purposeful young man, planning for his future. In the second book, *Irish Red,* Danny slowly takes the pole position in the family from his father, Ross; in many ways the book chronicles Danny's rise to full manhood, both in the woods, where he and Mike escape a cougar and save Ross from freezing to death, and in his new career, where he and Mike beat back a challenge from a cruel trainer and his English (horrors!) setters. By the third book, *Outlaw Red,* Danny is himself the authority figure to a new character, a backwoods boy euphoniously named Billy Dash, who is in many ways Danny Pickett again—a shy native woodsman who loves dogs inarticulately and loves Sean especially and wishes desperately that there might be a way for him to own Sean. Such a thing is not possible in the normal order of things, Billy being a kennel boy and Sean a show champion, but the end of *Outlaw Red,* much like the end of *Big Red,* finds boy and dog miraculously bound by mutual love and by Mr. Haggin's wise generosity.

A middle-aged man reads a boy's book much differently than he did when he was a boy, and where once I whipped through the books as fast as I could to find out what would happen, now I paused and pondered, and reread passages, and contemplated Kjelgaard at work. I noticed now, for example, that there are virtually no women in the books, and that the only woman who appears for more than a couple of sentences is a greedy, self-centered virago who tries to steal Red in the first book. (Two substantive females do play key roles in the trilogy, but they are canine: Sheila MacGuire, Red's mate, and Penelope of Killarney, called Penny, Sean's mate. Poor Mike remains a bachelor throughout his book, never even sniffing the possibility of love.) And I spent a lot of time contemplating Mr. Haggin, who is a sort of beneficent woods God, owning everything, adjudicating disputes, magisterially giving Red to Danny and Sean to Billy. A man could write a wonderfully obscure essay about the theology of *Big Red.*

In rereading, I also caught, here and there in vaguely remembered passages, tantalizing glimpses of myself at age ten. The middle-aged reader I am now, for example, realized that Danny's intimacy with the ways of the woods was something I yearned almost desperately for as a boy, despite my actual existence in a world of aluminum siding and asphalt and station wagons. Such a yearning had a lot to do with the coonskin cap and Davy Crockett and Daniel Boone craze of my 1960s boyhood, perhaps, and perhaps it also had a lot to do with membership in the Boy Scouts of America, an organization that sets out to teach elemental woodcraft, among other things (thrift, reverence, etc.), to its troops. Certainly in 1966, when I gobbled up the Red books, there were far fewer Danny Picketts in the American woods, and many fewer American woods, too, than there had been forty years previous, when Kjelgaard was himself a teenager watching marten chase squirrels through the beechwoods of the Alleghenies.

The general loss of woods and woodcraft may explain some of the enduring popularity of the *Red* books. I think that many young people—perhaps most young people—crave what wilderness they can find, if it is only rabbits among tract houses, or starlings in attics, or pigeons in ghettoes, or a tangled thicket in the yard, because youth is drawn intrinsically to the mystery of the natural world, the unregulated relentless procession of it, its life and death without adult supervision. That natural inclination may be more pronounced in an American youth because the lore and literature and history of this nation have so much of the outdoors in them: the deerslayers and primeval peoples of the eastern woods, the sodbusters and cowboys and horse-warriors of the plains and arid lands, the mountain men of the Rockies, the salmon tribes and loggers of the vast Northwest fir forests. And that inclination may be more pronounced still because what young people hear from every front these days is demise and loss, of forests, animals, ozone layers, ways of life. A boy on the edge of manhood, itching to be independent, soaked in stories of the woods and trails, interested as a matter of course in animals since he was an infant, frightened and saddened by the loss of much of the natural world—is it any wonder he might read *Big Red* avidly, so that for a time he would *be* Danny Pickett, woods-wise, walking silently through the forest, knowing the ways and manners of mysterious wolverines, lynx, marten, cougars, fishers? Half a century after Jim Kjelgaard invented Danny Pickett and set him to shambling through the woods in the opening lines of *Big Red*, those wild animals are no longer seen in the Allegheny beech forests where Kjelgaard walked as a boy, but the *Red* books sell as briskly as ever.

* * *

What I noticed above all, in rereading *Red*, was that it was more about animals in the woods than anything else, including maturing boys and show dogs, and this made me very interested in Kjelgaard the man. Here is a professional writer who diligently sets and follows plotlines but who talks with true love about traplines, who issues speech after speech about the great work that human beings do when they breed dogs but who is much more colorful and passionate when he talks about the terrific speed of a pine marten chasing a squirrel or the breeding seasons of red foxes ("my favorite animal, I think," he wrote to a friend late in life). How came this man, at age thirty-four, to be writing so knowledgeably about wolverines and lynx and the battle habits of huge black bears?

Born in 1910, in New York City, son of a physician, fourth of six children, Kjelgaard "was not yet out of three-cornered pants when the family moved to a farm in the Pennsylvania mountains," he wrote in 1951, in an autobiographical sketch for *The Junior Book of Authors.* "My father owned or acquired about 750 acres of land, which was stocked with cattle, horses, sheep, dogs, chickens, and everything else. Eventually our father sold the farm and we moved to Galeton, Pennsylvania [also in the Allegheny Mountains]. . . . Between intervals of attending school we ran trap lines, shot deer, and fished for trout." At age eighteen he enrolled at Syracuse University and lasted two years, after which he "held a dozen jobs, and at one time or another [was a] laborer, teamster, factory worker, plumber's apprentice, and surveyor's assistant. I started writing because things seemed just naturally to be heading in that direction anyhow."

A lovely last sentence, that one, funny and seemingly ingenuous; but that litany of jobs reveals a man unsure of his career, much like young Danny Pickett in *Big Red.* Perhaps Danny the young trapper and woodsman uncertain what to do in life came directly from Jim Kjelgaard in the same predicament in the same woods just before the Depression. It is interesting to note in this regard that Kjelgaard's first book, *Forest Patrol,* is about a young man in the Allegheny woods trying to decide what to do with his life; he decides to try for forest ranger school, a target Kjelgaard knew well, for his brother John had become a ranger.

Kjelgaard had a trapper's familiarity with *Mustelidae,* the carnivore family that features weasels at the small end, valuable fur-bearers such as mink, otter, marten, and fisher in the middle, and the king of the northern woods, the wolverine, at the top of the line. The clever, powerful, fearless wolverine is a fascinating creature (it figures prominently in the myths and lore of northern peoples, it has been known to attack and kill moose that outweigh it by nearly a ton, even grizzly bears and cougars cede kills to it, and it was and is renowned among trappers and hunters for robbing traplines and breaking into hunters' cabins for food), and an especially violent one plays a key role in *Big Red.* But Kjelgaard brings the whole *Mustelidae* family to the table in the three *Red* books, spending many pages explaining their lives and detailing how Danny sets traps for weasels (he nails fresh chicken heads to tree trunks and sets traps below, knowing that the weasel, hungry or not, will be drawn to blood), and mink and otter (water traps, carefully de-scented). As for marten, Kjelgaard uses this lithe, rare, arboreal creature to make a note of trapper ethics; Danny spots two marten while fishing in the mountains but he decides not to trap them as they are apparently the only pair in the region. Danny's is a far-sighted economic decision; leaving the marten to flourish might yield a steady supply in subsequent years. But I think too that Kjelgaard was a conservationist, and wanted to show his audience of postwar teenage boys that no trapping could be good trapping, and I also think he just liked writing about the marten, a little-known denizen of the deep woods.

Much of the fascination of the *Red* books, for me, was and is their casual knowledge about these and other mysterious mammals of the woods—the mustelids, bear, bobcat (or "wildcat," as Ross calls them), lynx, cougar. For a boy like me, growing up in suburban New York where wilderness was sparse and the only unmapped places were the miles of rippling dunes along Long Island's Atlantic shore, Ross's offhand mention (in *Big Red*) of "the fisher cat we pulled spit-ting out of a cave last year" was entrancing. The phrase reeked of independence, woodcraft, an easy familiarity with the most elusive creatures of the North American forests. The chances of me actually seeing a marten or fisher in the thin woods near me were beyond nil, but there was something in me that wanted very much to be able to know a creature like a marten, and understand its life among the high branches, and recognize it instantly, as Danny does, when he looks up into the beech branches and notes a terrified squirrel flee-ing from "a lithe brown creature, fully as agile and tree-wise as the squirrel, its silky coat glistening in the sun."

Rereading *Red*, I realized too that I owe a debt to Kjelgaard: He set me on a path toward other writers, many of them superb. Entranced by his knowledge of the woods and woods-creatures, I turned first to other books about mustelids, like Gavin Maxwell's fine *Ring of Bright Water* and Henry Williamson's *Tarka* (both about otters, and the latter, interestingly, T. E. Lawrence's favorite book), and Kenneth Grahame's *The Wind in the Willows,* starring Badger and an army of villainous weasels, and Cameron Langford's *The Winter of the Fisher.* From there I journeyed into such popular naturalists as Edwin Way Teale and Charlton Ogburn and Hal Borland and Roger Tory

Peterson, and as the years went on I developed a natural bent toward the many excellent writers in whose works animals are integral or central: John Burroughs, Gilbert White, John Muir, Henry Beston, T. H. White, John Baker, Rachel Carson, John McPhee, Annie Dillard, Barry Lopez (in whose work there are many wolverines), John and Frank Craighead, Ann Zwinger, Peter Matthiessen, Terry Tempest Williams, Richard Nelson, William deBuys, Robert Michael Pyle, dozens more. And from those writers I went further into the context of animals—books about landscape, zoology, geology, ornithology, paleontology. Not only have I thus been introduced to some of the most imaginative and interesting American literature ever written, but those writers and their books have led in part to my own interests as a man and as a writer, and for this delightful education I must thank, before all other writers, the "laborer, teamster, factory worker, plumber's apprentice, and surveyor's assistant" who "started writing because things seemed just naturally to be heading in that direction anyhow."

* * *

Even as I acknowledge my debt I am bound to confess that Kjelgaard has many flaws as a writer. His characters are simple at best and cartoons at worst. It could be argued, successfully, that the Irish setters are more complete characters than any of the human beings except Danny, and that Danny is really the only fully drawn human character in the books, Ross and Mr. Haggin and Billy Dash and others serving as foils. And Danny is only fully drawn, I suspect, because Kjelgaard was writing about himself with rueful affection.

At his best his books could rise to the level of *Big Red,* which is as much about Danny's rite of passage from boy to man as it is about the setters, and which features nonstop action and plot progress; at his worst he cranked out stories that, read several at a time, begin to appear to be made by recipe. His range was, by evidence of his books, somewhat limited. His books were very nearly all about hunting, dogs, or animals, very often a combination of the three, as in the *Big Red* trilogy, and a slew of his books starred a single wild animal: a beaver, a fox, a bobcat, a deer, a moose, a polar bear, a coyote. But it could just as easily be said that the man knew his talents better than most and rode those talents hard and well. Kjelgaard was also a serious student of history and wrote books about prehistoric man, about Australian aborigines, about the American frontier, about the Oregon Trail, and the self-explanatory *Explorations of Pere Marquette, Story of Geronimo, Coming of the Mormons,* and *We Were There at the Oklahoma Land Run.*

Kjelgaard was a writer whose books nearly always featured "an engaging animal, a colorful person, and a distinctive habitat," as Karen Hoyle noted in *Twentieth-Century Children's Writers.* And it would be a sniffy critic who cannot admire the facts that Kjelgaard knew the woods and its denizens intimately, wrote about them without sentimentality and portentous symbolism, and had the rare ability to rivet adolescents with his prose. Those virtues, especially that elusive last one which can spark an entire lifetime's itch to read, are nothing to sneer at.

Reading a masterpiece like Barry Lopez's *Arctic Dreams* after reading the *Red* books is like encountering a bear in the deep woods after setting out from a clearing filled with chittering squirrels, but the large blessing is a cousin to the smaller one, and each is a bit of grace, and so as I shuffle happily through many books and the deep fir and cedar forests of the Pacific Northwest, I often think with affection of Kjelgaard, and imagine him late in a fall afternoon in his beloved Allegheny beechwoods, walking with "the shuffling, loose-kneed gait of the born woodsman" that he bestowed upon Danny at the very beginning of *Big Red.*

With Kjelgaard in my mind are his dogs, Irish setters of course, snuffling after rabbits, bedeviling woodchucks that barely haul their fat autumn selves into their holes as the dogs snap at their heels. The sun is splattering down between the branches of the trees. Perhaps two dead grouse are swinging at the man's belt and his rifle is carried loosely in his arm as he heads for home and dinner, roast grouse over rice, and after dinner a stiff cup of coffee and a couple of hours writing up the way that bobcat over north of the mountain doubled back through a laurel thicket to fool the dogs, which are at the moment snuffling themselves to sleep in front of the fire. Tomorrow morning maybe he will hike out to the pond and watch for mink and otter, and then in the afternoon work some on the book about a red fox. But right now the sun is low and the day is done and the woods are filled with stories.

# CHAPTER EIGHT

# Greeneland

I have just emerged from an immersion of some weeks in the works of the wonderful English novelist (and memoirist, essayist, travel writer, film critic, screenwriter, playwright, and short-story maker) Graham Greene. With the urbane Mr. Greene as guide I traveled to Istanbul, Liberia, Mexico, Estonia, England, Hollywood, Cuba, Panama, and South America. I read stories and essays, novels and film criticism, accounts of his adventures and misadventures, stories of his opium smoking, stories of the libel lawsuit brought against him by Miss Shirley Temple. (Greene had hinted, broadly, that her performance in a film was thinly veiled pandering.) I read a great deal by him and nothing about him, on the theory that the best guide to a writer's peculiar and particular country is the map he has left behind himself in his prose.

Some conclusions:

He was perhaps the most prolific fine writer of this century.

He was a past master at creating the sub-sub-character, the character whose job is simply to move the plot along but who, in Greene's hands, takes on a sudden vibrant life of his or her own.

He was obsessed with secrecy and shifting identities to the point where a diligent reader wonders (a) if there really *was* such a person as Graham Greene, and (b) how many other fine novelists and storytellers draw upon their own fascination with other selves to create the characters in their books—which are, in so many cases, other selves.

\* \* \*

Prolixity first. For a man who maintained he would rather not have been a writer ("Often I have wished that [my] future had been a district office in Sierra Leone and twelve tours of malarial duty and a finishing dose of blackwater fever when the danger of retirement approached"), he wrote an incredible amount of prose—more than thirty novels, entertainments, stories, and plays, two travel books, two reluctant autobiographies, perhaps a thousand essays, articles, and literary reviews, and an entire book of film criticism.

His literary criticism alone shows a stunning breadth: He wrote penetrating essays about such disparate figures as Beatrix Potter, Colette, Rider Haggard, Hans Christian Andersen, Francis Parkman, John Buchan, Samuel Butler, Georges Bernanos, François Mauriac, Ford Madox Ford, and H. H. Munro (Saki), as well as on canonical stalwarts like Conrad, Fielding, Sterne, Shakespeare, Dickens, Waugh, Stevenson, Kipling, Chesterton, and Simone Weil. There is a great deal to be said for reading Greene on, say, Rider Haggard (whom he admired), but in an odd way it is the film criticism that I found most interesting, partly for its sheer scope—it's doubtful that Greene missed seeing a motion picture made between 1920 and 1960—and partly for the Shirley Temple brouhaha, in which Greene was found guilty of slander. The suit—which Miss Temple reportedly knew nothing about and during which Greene refused to appear in court—was a minor affair, but I continue to relish the thought of the ebullient, apple-cheeked flower of American girlhood at odds with the sallow and urbane English master of hidden identities. Life provides so few moments of pure delight that when one appears it tends to stay in the mind, if not in a London courtroom.

\* \* \*

Perhaps Greene's greatest accomplishment as a novelist is his creation of vibrant and mysterious sub-sub-characters—Lopez in *Our Man in Havana*, the dog Buller in *The Human Factor*, the anonymous ship captain in the opening of *A Burnt-Out Case*. These characters are in a curious category—more than quick sketches, such as the limping beggar who frames *Our Man in Havana* with an opening and closing appearance, but less than heroes, heroines, and supporting players. (A whole and delightful other essay might be written about Greene's third, fourth, and fifth characters—how very many of them are doctors, for example, or the many ways in which he wields priests as lesser characters.) They are essentially plot devices, created to move the story forward, but they have a relentless, squirming life of their own—a life, one senses dimly, not at all confined by what little Greene chose to put on paper.

Señor Lopez is a good example. He is a mere shop assistant in *Our Man in Havana;* his role is to represent Business, to be a human example of the dusty profession (vacuum cleaner sales) pursued, desultorily, by Mr. Wormold, the anti-hero. Lopez appears here and there throughout the book, here showing a vacuum cleaner to a prospective customer, here closing up shop, but his role is less active than representative; he is holding down the vacuum cleaner fort, such as it is, while Mr. Wormold is sucked inevitably into the far-cical and savage netherworld of spydom. So Lopez is an anchor, a paper man whose presence covers Mr. Wormold's total lack of con-cern for his livelihood.

Yet Lopez is *alive*—eerily so. In one scene Mr. Wormold contem-plates recruiting his assistant as a secret agent, and in Greene's hands the very brief scene tells a penetrating tale of this unimpor-tant character. Lopez—who cannot pronounce his boss's name even after many years of employ, and who calls him Vormell, Vomell, and Ommel, respectively—misunderstands the offer completely.

"This will be confidential work, for me personally, you under-stand," says Wormold.

"Ah yes, *señor.* Personal services I understand. You can trust me. I am discreet. Of course I will say nothing to the *señorita* [Wormold's daughter Milly].

"I think perhaps you *don't* understand . . ."

"When a man reaches a certain age, he no longer wishes to search for a woman himself, he wishes to rest from trou-ble," continues Lopez, sure of his ground now. "He wishes to command, 'Tonight yes, tomorrow night no.' To give his directions to someone he trusts . . ."

"I don't mean anything of the kind. What I was trying to say—well, it had nothing to do . . ."

"You do not need to be embarrassed in speaking to me, *Señor Vormole.* I have been with you many years."

On it goes, and Wormold finally gives up, but Lopez, the dusty plot prop, has surged to life, planning assignations, philosophizing about changes in lust and love as the body ages, and politely man-gling his employer's name again and again.

This sort of startling life in parts of the set is what sets Greene apart from not only other "Catholic novelists" but from most of the finest novelists of our century—even colossi like William Faulkner.

I am not saying that Greene is a "better" novelist than Faulkner—or Walker Percy, J. F. Powers, Flannery O'Connor, David Plante, Georges Bernanos, François Mauriac, Andre Dubus, Mary Gordon, George Higgins, Annie Dillard, or John L'Heureux, to mention a handful of writers who are or were Catholic—but I do say that he had more *reach* than any of them, that the vast layers of his characters are all alive, more so than in any other novelist I can think of. George Higgins' mean streeters come close, but Higgins, undisputed master of dialogue as character code, doesn't have mystery infusing his books like Greene does. Greene's scenes always seem to be corners of larger scenes, and while our attention is deftly focused on the foreground, the background drifts along half-noticed, half-understood.

I also say that Greene wrote more in more genres. I say he managed to pursue his analysis of good and evil and the vagaries of trust and will, his eternal obsession with identity and escape from identity, with greater skill than anyone else writing prose in the twentieth century. I say that he ranks among the very best writers of our time, Catholic or secular, English or American or Kenyan or Peruvian.

\* \* \*

It is an almost irresistible temptation to rank and categorize writers. There is something immensely pleasurable in stacking them one against another, in the same way that we arrange sports stars and musicians and actors against their past and present colleagues. Perhaps this is a groping attempt to understand their astonishing skills, and identify those characteristics that make them magicians and make us awed members of the audience, open-mouthed as the flames shoot upward and the doves explode from the hat; perhaps it is also a means of understanding them by reduction—talking about Greene as a Catholic novelist, for example, takes him away from the noisy multitude of all writers and places him in the rarefied company of his fellow religionists, and seeing him shoulder-to-shoulder with fewer people may make the outline of his genius a little easier to see.

But such reduction is both false and misleading, for at least two reasons. One is that pigeonholing is almost always unedifying and irrelevant; the other is that I think there is no such thing as a Catholic writer.

Irrelevancy first. With the possible exception of the language in which a novel is written, does any other information about origin matter to the quality of the story? Does it matter that the author of *Smilla's Sense of Snow* is Danish? Does it really matter to the quality of *Jazz* that Toni Morrison is black? Does it matter when reading Annie Dillard's *The Living* that the author is a convert to Catholicism? If the act of reading a novel is the central transaction between writer and reader, as I think it is, then all other information about the writer is gossip at best and limiting at worst.

I was once roundly scolded, rightly so, for writing that the polymath American Wallace Stegner was a "Western writer." The scolder, a friend of mine and an astute reader, pointed out that forcing Stegner into a single region was a great disservice to him; the man's work ranged far afield in every sense, and making him a regional phenomenon was aiding and abetting the booksellers who jammed Stegner in with Zane Grey as a writer of dust devils and horse operas. This is a disservice by no means restricted to novelists, by the way; such superb writers as Barry Lopez, Edward Abbey, Peter Matthiessen, and Edward Hoagland suffer from the generic label "nature writer," a tag that intrigues fewer prospective readers than it frightens off, I suspect.

As for "Catholic writer," I don't believe there is such an animal. There are writers who happen to be Catholic—Andre Dubus, say. There are writers like John L'Heureux or Barry Lopez whose "subject . . . is the action of grace in territory largely held by the devil," as Flannery O'Connor said of her own work. There are writers like the late J. F. Powers who use a nearly exclusively Catholic milieu. There are writers like David Plante who, as he says, "prepare[s] for grace to occur in my work." And there were writers like Walker Percy and Graham Greene, who used Catholicism as the sub-language of a novel, whether in deed (movies as mock sacraments in Percy's *The Moviegoer*) or character (the whiskey priest in Greene's masterpiece, *The Power and the Glory*).

Greene, a convert to Catholicism, did not believe that his faith affected his books, other than possibly giving him an informed basis upon which to portray priests, and he additionally did not believe there was any such thing as a Catholic writer. Writers were writers, to their joy or regret, and their faiths, like their nationalities and their preferences for sex, wine, and literature, were wells from which to draw more accurate truths—although the inaccuracy of truth was one of his persistent themes.

\* \* \*

There are other matters which set Greene apart. The odd limpidity of his form, for example; I found, after reading a slew of his novels one after another, that his stage-work was transparent but that it did not matter. That is to say, I could easily see his hand moving characters in and out of my view, changing the backdrop, etc., but that this sensibility to the novelist at work did not detract from the power of the story. *The Orient Express* is a good example. Within the first thirty pages or so a reader is perfectly aware that Greene is using the train's journey as a chapter device, and using the train's disparate population as a character device; yet the story remains riveting, because it is in the hands of a fledgling master storyteller. Much later in life Greene returned to the travel motif in *Travels with my Aunt* and a comparison of the books is revelatory of the progress of his craft. The first book teems with characters whose stories are painstakingly woven together as much as possible; the second is a much more streamlined account in which travel serves to simply shift scenes in which the central character remains.

And while one may argue that Greene was perennially concerned with shifting morality, shifting selves, and "ways of escape," as he titled his second autobiography, one is also forced to admit that no Greene book is like another; and in a writer who commits thirty books, that is a startling and rare accomplishment. Even a superb writer like Joseph Conrad, to name another British novel factory, returned so often to similar settings and themes and character types that *Almayer's Folly* and *Tales of Unrest*, for example, might easily be considered sequential volumes in a six-volume work entitled, perhaps, *A Study of Native and Colonial Human Character in the Malaysian Archipelago, with Especial Attention Paid to the Seafaring Classes.*

Thus to say that Greene wrote "espionage novels," for example, is nonsense. There really are no spy novels by Greene—*The Human Factor*, which traces the manner in which a quiet desk officer in the British Secret Service is forced to betray his employer, is not at all like *Our Man in Havana*, which traces the ways in which Wormold is persuaded to join, and betray, the British Secret Service. Nor is *The Orient Express* (published initially under Greene's own title, *The Stambul Train*), which is a chase novel, anything at all like *The Power and the Glory*, in which a defrocked priest is chased throughout the book, or like *A Burnt-Out Case*, in which a man's fame chases him relentlessly even as he seeks, unsuccessfully, to elude both his former fame and the former self that earned worldly honor.

My point is that Greene was writing about men and women and their true or false hearts, not about spy machinery or the hierarchy of the Church or the British criminal class. That he wrote about hearts is why he was a great novelist. That is what great novelists do. There are other reasons they are great—they choose fascinating milieus for their tales, they have a genius for inventing real people (other selves?), they are able to echo the ways that we really talk, they tell stories with pace and mystery, they distill in a particular character a whole era or a classic human type—a Mister Micawber, an Ahab, an Emma Bovary.

But the reason that the novel is finally the greatest and most popular literary genre is because at its best it is both story and symbolic lesson. We live by stories, they are the foods that sustain and nourish us, from nursery tales to the stories, true and false, we tell our lovers, to the stories of us left behind in the mouths and hearts of family and friends. From cradle to grave we tell stories and are sustained and created by them; indeed those who believe in religious stories also believe that they will quite literally be saved by them. These are the most ludicrous and wonderful stories I have ever heard, and many is the day I wish I could meet their authors. Perhaps someday I will. Perhaps Mr. Greene will be nearby, smoking, smiling his enigmatic smile, locked in animated discussion with Miss Shirley Temple.

CHAPTER NINE

# Mr. Joyce

Men and women all over the world gather on June 16 every year, in celebration of the fictive adventures of a Jewish Irishman, because on that day in 1904 a young man named James Augustine Aloysius Joyce, age twenty-two, met a Galway girl named Nora Barnacle, age twenty, at Merrion Square in Dublin and walked out to Ringsend with her on their first date. He'd first seen her a week before, as he sauntered down Nassau Street—a tall, attractive, red-haired girl who answered his shy greeting with what he thought remarkable self-possession. Instantly smitten, he asked her out walking; and years later, when he conceived his great novel of Dublin life, he offered Nora the eloquent compliment of setting the whole novel on that day, June 16, 1904.

It should be noted that Nora did not acknowledge the compliment with all the grace she could muster: She read only twenty-seven pages of *Ulysses* before putting it down forever as unreadable. "Why don't you write books that people can read?" said the Galway girl to the Dublin boy.

The Joyce family hailed ultimately from an ancient clan in Galway, but John Joyce, James's father, was a Cork City man. Renowned in his youth for his great skill as a hunter and bon vivant after the hunt, he was also famous for his meticulous knowledge of the country—"there is not a field in County Cork that I do not know," he boasted. He started at university—Queen's College in Cork—with a bang, quickly becoming a star student, athlete, and legendary singer in college musicals, but soon enough he was flunking out since he spent all his time in theaters and pubs. Away he went to Dublin to start over. He found lodgings in south Dublin, entered politics, found a job at a distillery, and continued to sing so well that he was said to be the greatest tenor in Ireland. He also sang on Sundays at the Church of the Three Patrons in Rathgar, and there in the choir he met a beautiful blonde girl named Mary Jane Murray, of Murrays

from County Longford. They were married in 1880. In the next thirteen years John and Mary made fourteen children, of whom ten
survived; the oldest was James, named for a long line of James Joyces
stretching back in the family into Galway.

James was educated mostly by the Jesuits, in Kildare and Dublin,
and went on to University College in Dublin, where he established a
firm reputation as a fine writer, omnivorous reader, big drinker, and
youth of remarkable rudeness and arrogance; he told Yeats, whom
he had essentially begged for an audience, that Yeats' poetry was too
bound up in nature and that Yeats was too old to be educated by the
friendship of young Mister Joyce. After college he tried on a few
careers, each for a month or so: doctor (he applied to medical school
in Dublin and Paris), singer (he took lessons and won prizes, but
disliked the long hours of daily practice), schoolteacher in Dalkey,
and—loopiest of all—traveling lute-player and singer of ballads, a
scheme that failed because he couldn't afford the lute. Then came
June of 1904, and Miss Nora Barnacle, who thought the impertinent
young man who stopped her on Nassau Street was a Swedish sailor,
because of his yachting cap and piercing blue eyes.

More than anything else when young, James Joyce wanted to be a
professional singer on the stage. He wanted to be, in fact, John
McCormack, who was then just beginning his world fame, and the
high point of Joyce's musical career was later that same summer, in
August, when he actually sang with McCormack—and, I note cheerfully, a Mister J. C. Doyle—on the final night of Horse Show Week.
The concert, held at the Antient Concert Rooms in Dublin (where
his father had sung thirty years before), was a mixed success—the
singers went on late, the crowd was "noisy and irritable," and the
young Miss Reilly accompanying the singers on the piano abruptly
left the stage and did not return. Joyce then sat down at the piano
and accompanied himself on three songs, earning himself the plau-
dits "artistic," "emotional," "charming," and "tender and sweet" in
the next day's newspaper. A friend said of his beautiful voice that it
was "pure Irish, filled with tenderness, melancholy, and bitterness."
His tender and melancholy voice also charmed his new lover, who
confided to friends years later, in her characteristically blunt way,
that "Jim should have stuck to music instead of bothering with the
writing."

\* \* \*

But he didn't stick with the music, other than as a parlor entertainment, and he did stick with the writing, as he and Nora (and eventually their two children Giorgio and Lucia) moved first to Austria and then to Italy, Switzerland, France, and back again to Zurich, where Joyce died in 1941. At his brief funeral, on a snowy hill not far from the city zoo, a tenor sang Monteverdi.

During his fifty-eight years on the planet Joyce wrote one of everything: first a book of precious little poems called *Chamber Music*, which is terrible; then a book of crisp, perfect, short stories called *Dubliners*, which is superb; then an essentially orthodox autobiographical novel called *Portait of the Artist as a Young Man*, which is excellent but primly self-conscious; then a play called *Exiles*, which is not good; then a vast unorthodox novel called *Ulysses*, which is terrific; then a nearly unimaginably vast creative act called *Finnegans Wake*, which is admirable for its ambition—its heroine is the river Liffey, and the entire book is built as a circle so that the end leads back into the opening sentences—but, as a readable narrative, is essentially incomprehensible.

What was Joyce after in his work? In short, the astonishing miracle of every minute. "Don't you think there is a certain resemblance between the mystery of the Mass and what I am trying to do?" he once asked his brother Stanislaus. "I mean that I am trying to give people some kind of intellectual pleasure or spiritual enjoyment by converting the bread of everyday life into something that has a permanent artistic life of its own, for their mental, moral, and spiritual uplift." This theme of transformation, of miraculous revelation, of secular transubstantiation, appears throughout his work; the sudden "revelation of the whatness of a thing," the moment in which "the soul of the commonest object seems to us radiant," in "sudden spiritual manifestation," says his most autobiographical character, Stephen Daedalus. In another conversation with his brother, Joyce asked, "Do you see that man who has just skipped out of the way of the tram? Consider, if he had been run over, how significant every act of his would at once become. I don't mean for the police inspector. I mean for anybody who knew him. And his thoughts, for anybody who could know them. It is my idea of the significance of trivial things that I want to give the two or three unfortunate wretches who may eventually read me."

More than two or three wretches eventually read this most unusual man. He was deeply superstitious, deeply frightened of and delighted by the smallest events as omens. He fainted in despair at seeing a rat in the street. He expressed great satisfaction in the good omen that *Ulysses* was published on his fortieth birthday, although he had arranged that himself, indeed insisted on it to his exhausted publisher. He was terrified of dogs and madness. He was so terrified of thunderstorms that this most bitter of ex-Catholics would, upon hearing the rolling roar of thunder, instantly make a Sign of the Cross and mutter *Jesus of Nazareth, King of the Jews, from a sudden and unprovided-for death deliver us, O Lord*, a habit which mortified him. He was legendarily lazy and opined that every room ought to have a bed in it. He drank a bottle of wine a night, often two, at the local cafés in Paris and Rome where he sat quietly in the corner listening to the patrons and asking people about their lives. "I never met a bore," he said once, trying to explain his extraordinary capacity for listening, and indeed his greatest genius may have been his infinite ability to listen to, and remember, the particular cadences and specific stories of every sort of person he encountered: "waiters, tellers, fruitsellers, hotel porters, concierges, bank clerks," as his biographer Richard Ellmann says.

For all his considerable pride in his art, and very nearly arrogant conviction that the best office performable by his friends, family, and fans was to provide him with steady money and good company, he was relentlessly honest about what he wanted to do in his work— show the ordinary to be extraordinary—and about himself. "Don't make a hero out of me," he said to a friend singing his praises. "I'm only a simple middle-class man." And to Carl Jung, of all people, he summed himself simply as "a man of small virtue, inclined to extravagance and alcoholism."

All true; he was often cruel and cold, he was eternally in debt and eternally on the prowl for loans, and he drank an ocean of wine, often dancing home from the cafés near dawn. (Always white wine, which he called "electricity," never red, or "beefsteak.") But his courage in the face of encroaching blindness, constant financial worry, his daughter's serious mental illness, and worldwide vituperation of his greatest work was admirable indeed; and for all his famous and almost-true remark that a razed Dublin could be rebuilt from the city captured whole in his books, his greatest accomplishment was to make the quotidian astonishing, the commonplace uncommon.

For millennia before Joyce, literature had bent toward the doings of the heroic, the great, and the saintly, using the lives and works of the high-born or military to entertain and instruct the many; but the quiet man from Rathgar, the "simple middle-class man," bent the world's literature the other way, toward the untold doings of the unknown many, making epic sagas of everyday life. His was the greatest literary work of our century, and in my mind Jimmy Joyce, born in south Dublin, is one of the handful of greatest writers ever, in any language.

Of his many works many will be forgotten, some deservedly so— but his collection of stories about Dubliners is perfect, and his immense embrace of a novel, set on the day he met his wife ("Barnacle's her name? Ah, she'll never leave him," said his father when he heard of the affair) is, to use that most enticing of adjectives, unique. It is also hilarious, heart-breaking, and stunningly ambitious. I do not believe there is another book that comes so close to catching the infinite whirl and roar of horrible and joyous stories, the holy minutiae of our lives, between covers.

It is instructive to learn that Joyce fussed endlessly over the proper color of those covers when the book was first printed; he wanted the perfect shade of blue—the color, he said, of the sea. A suitable and subtle advertisement for the oceanic contents therein.

# CHAPTER TEN

# Deeper Water

The best songwriter you never heard of has recorded fifteen albums of his work and sold a million records and played live for two million people. Perhaps thirty million people have savored his songs around the world. He has toured Europe, Australia, Scandinavia, and North America. He has toured with Bob Dylan and Ani DiFranco and Joe Jackson. He is so popular in his native country that a dozen female singers there have made a tribute record of their versions of his songs. He has been officially named Songwriter of the Year in his country. *Rolling Stone* has called him "one of the finest songwriters ever." He has been called his country's Bruce Springsteen, Elvis Costello, Bruce Cockburn, and Ray Davies. He has been called "the people's poet" of his nation. He has composed and performed the scores of films. He has produced records and written songs for dozens of other singers, among them members of his country's ravaged original people. He has published a collection of his lyrics, now in its second edition. While he has written many dozens of love songs, like every songwriter ever born, he has also, unlike every singer ever born, written songs about alcoholism and murder and lust and fading love and prison and jealousy and red rage and savage politics and courage of every shape and stripe from that of tribal leaders to that of single mothers. His songs in toto are so popular in his country that recently a collection of his greatest hits was released which immediately became his best-selling record ever and caused him, as he says, "to blush when I hear them in coffee shops over the public address. I turn and slip out. Your old songs are ships that sail away from you."

Yet the people's poet of his country, one of the finest songwriters ever, opened his 2002 tour of North America in a dank hole of a bar in Seattle, where he and his crack band earned $2,587 (before expenses) from 199 paying patrons for an incendiary two-hour show. Before the concert he signed ten autographs and after the show twenty people waited in line to shake his hand, press cassettes of their music on him, thank him for songs that rang daily in their hearts, or invite him out for a beer.

Finally, at about three in the morning, on the first wet day of spring in the Pacific Northwest, the best songwriter you never heard of and his four bandmates walked up glistening silent Blanchard Street to a bland motor inn, the first of fifteen such modest accommodations the band would stay in during their six-week tour, as they traveled in their eight-bunk bus from Washington state to Washington city, from Edmonton to Austin, from Louisville to Los Angeles, from universal acclaim at home to somewhere between cult and stardom in North America.

* * *

His greatest ambition as a child was to play professional football or cricket. At about age seventeen, he says, it became clear to him that he was not going to play professional football or cricket, so he took off traveling for a year, from Hobart to Darwin to Fremantle, working odd jobs along the way. One job was as a "silver boy" on the Indian Pacific Railroad from Port Pirie to Kalgoorlie, on the Adelaide-Perth line, "washing and hand-drying knives and forks for three meal-sittings a day, for *very* particular bosses." Then he tried college for a term, at Flinders University in Adelaide. Then he worked on a railroad line in Queensland, as a "fettler," or jack-of-all-trades laborer.

Somewhere along the line there, between Port Pirie and Kalgoorlie and Queensland, the young man who had played the piano as a boy and the trumpet as an adolescent and the air guitar on a tennis racket started fooling around with a real guitar, getting good enough to play Australian and American folk songs in bars, and early in 1976 he wrote his own song. It was a brief thing, "only the four lines," as he says, but it mattered greatly to him at age twenty, because it was the first time he'd composed his own music and set his own poem to it, in such a way that the words and the riff became a small joined story:

It's the falling apart that makes you
It's the running around that breaks you
It's the going down that wakes you
It's the riding of trains that takes you

So was born, with this little train quatrain, the great Australian songwriter Paul Kelly, who subsequently moved to Sydney and Melbourne, wrote two hundred more (and longer) songs, and became the people's poet of the Antipodes. Yet for all those songs and all those years learning to write them, for all that he has spent a quarter of a century learning to immediately snatch the scraps of melody that pop into his head and hum or strum them into a tape recorder and then later find the words that fit the melody and shape them with his bandmates and producers and engineers, when a song is *born*—when the melody leads to a chorus and the words pour into both and there suddenly is a new song in the world where it never was before—Kelly still, at age forty-seven, feels like falling to his knees in gratitude that it happened again. "I only know a few basic chords and I set out to write songs about little things, dumb things," he says. "It's a funky, chancy, mysterious process. I still feel like a total beginner. Every time a song happens it seems like a miracle to me."

\* \* \*

Kelly was born in Adelaide, "one of nine, though the third died, leaving us eight: Anne, Sheila, Martin, John, me, Mary Jo, David, and Tony. Josephine died as a baby so I never knew her. We all played the piano as children, my parents made us all learn it, and I was first-chair trumpet in high school, though I must confess there were only three trumpet players in all the school. We were Catholic and I was an altar boy. Our school was run by the Christian Brothers. My dad, John, was of Irish ancestry and my mum, Josephine, was of Italian stock, so we had the double Catholic whammo, and also the Irish and Italian and Australian and Catholic attitude to visitors and food—the house is open and all are welcome and there's always good food on the table. There were always big family gatherings and picnics at the races or at the national park nearby. I remember camping in the Adelaide Hills a couple of miles from where we lived. I remember my dad drinking beer out of a pewter mug at picnics. I remember that vividly. He died when I was thirteen, and he'd had Parkinson's disease for years before he died, so I remember him as frail, not a dad you could kick a ball with."

Dad's hands used to shake but I never knew he was dying
I was thirteen I never dreamed he could fall

And all the great-aunts were red in the eyes from crying
I rang the bells I never felt nothing at all
All the king's horses and all the king's men
Cannot bring him back again

John Kelly was the great-grandson of Jeremiah Kelly, who fled Ireland and its horrendous famine for Australia in 1852. Jeremiah settled north of Adelaide in the town of Clare, named for the western Irish county and filled with fellow exiles from *An Gorta Mor,* the Hunger Great. There he married Mary Baker and they farmed. Their first few years were years of good rain, but then the rains declined and "the true dry nature of the land revealed itself," as Jeremiah's great-great-grandson observes, and soon enough the Kellys were residents of the city of Adelaide, where Jeremiah begat James who begat Frank who begat John who begat Paul. The Biblical chime of this sentence is apt: among the songs Jeremiah's great-great-grandson most enjoys playing really loud in concert is his ferocious rocker "Love Is The Law," the lyrics of which are drawn entirely from Saint Paul's letter to the Corinthians.

Though I speak in tongues of angels
And in many tongues of men
Though prophecy may sing through me
Without love I'm nothing
Love is the law, the law is love

"My dad read Greek and Latin," says Paul. "He was a lawyer, a business colleague of the great cricket star Sir Don Bradman, and he loved languages and music. He was always listening to the Brandenburg Concerto in his study on Sunday. He wasn't musical himself, couldn't carry a tune. My mother, however, played the piano and sang beautifully. Her parents had been opera singers. Her father was Count Ercole Filippini, who was born in Milan and was a baritone at La Scala, and her mother was the first woman to conduct a symphony orchestra in Australia. Ercole Filippini was singing with a Spanish opera company, the Gonzales Brothers, on a tour of Australia when the First World War broke out, and he stayed in Australia and became a singing teacher in Sydney and fell in love with one of his students, Miss Anne McParland—my grandmother. A friend of mine wants to turn this story into an opera and has asked me to write the music for it.

"My mother was a loving, funny, patient woman who'd been wild and lovely in her youth—she'd been engaged four times, once for one night only. She ruled us gently, though you knew quite well when you were in trouble; she'd wear what we called the Look of Death. She sang to us on car trips, a different song for each of us, popular songs into which she'd slip our names and twist some of the lyrics to be about us. Tony's song had an ice-cream cart in it, I remember. I shared a room with my brothers, so I remember snatches of our songs. And my mom and dad would read to all of us, and we all said the rosary together every night, on our knees. At my mum's wake we all said the rosary together again—the first time in years we'd all prayed it together."

In her last years Josephine Kelly lived in Brisbane and her children and their children visited in packs and gaggles. She sang, she played the piano, she went to church, she cared for her own mother until Anne's death at age ninety-six. Josephine's favorite pastime was Scrabble.

"She was a demon Scrabble player, a master at it, and very competitive," says Paul. "The last game we played I was way up with a couple of tiles to go, as close to winning as you can get—and I rarely beat her—when with her last tiles she put down *qi*, and informed me that it was the new accepted spelling of a word meaning the life force. She knew all sorts of obscure two-letter words like that for exactly that reason. Triple letter score on the *q*, going two ways, she wins. Two days later she died."

Josephine was cremated after she died, and in typical Kelly family fashion, says Paul, the clan dithered around as to what to do with her ashes. There was talk of burying her ashes with her husband John in Adelaide, or scattering them somewhere else, but in the end they decided not to decide right away. A year passed. Finally the funeral parlor in Brisbane called Martin and asked firmly for a decision as to his mother's ashes. Martin drove his mother's ashes home, belted into the front passenger seat, talking to her the whole way home.

"Oddly enough my mum's favorite song of mine was 'Somebody's Forgetting Somebody,'" says Paul.

In the years after her husband's death and before her own, Josephine Kelly often remarked to her children that she hoped to get to heaven more to cradle her husband's face again than to see the face of God: "God second, John first," as she said. Remembering that remark, her third son wrote a song called "I Close My Eyes and

Think of You" and played it for her one afternoon in the Brisbane
hospital where she spent her last weeks.

When another day has ended
And everything's been said and done
And the lights across the valley
All go out one by one
I close my eyes and think of you.

I know there's a singing river
I've heard about the golden shore
But I would pass by all that beauty
Just to be with you once more.

* * *

In 1976, after writing his train quatrain, Paul Kelly set about the
enormously difficult work of trying to make a living as a musician.
He moved to Melbourne and played in bars and clubs and theaters.
He learned to play acoustic guitar and then electric guitar and then
harmonica. He played house parties and weddings and bars. He
played reunions and parties and receptions and anniversaries and
ribbon-cuttings and bars. He learned his craft. He started a band,
the Dots, and made two records as Paul Kelly and the Dots that he
doesn't officially count now among his records (*Talk* and *Manilla*,
both out of print) and then, in 1984, struck up with a gaggle of
Melbourne musicians who would become collectively the Coloured
Girls: the late guitarist Steve Connolly, drummer Mick Barclay,
bassist Jon Schofield, keyboard player Peter Bull, and on the saxophone occasionally, sounding eerily like Clarence Clemons, Chris
Coyne.

The Coloured Girls played "all kinds of places, from leaky base-
ment bars to marble and velvet theaters," as Paul says, smiling. In
1985 he and Connolly and Barclay went to Sydney and recorded
*Post*, a lean and largely acoustic song cycle that included "Adelaide"
(a bittersweet paean to his hometown) and "From St. Kilda to King's
Cross" (an elegy to Melbourne). A year later the whole band
recorded a twenty-four-song double album called *Gossip*, and things
were different ever after.

"For one thing I could pay my bills after *Gossip;* that was the first
year I actually made a living as a musician," says Kelly. "Thirty years

old and finally turned a profit. The thing about that record, though, wasn't the money, such as it was, it was the play—it got *played,* and people *heard* it. I'll always remember hearing 'Before Too Long' on the radio for the first time with the Coloured Girls as we drove to a show and turning the volume waaaaaay up."

*Gossip* also displayed the full range of Paul Kelly songs: ballads, rockers, rave-ups, songs with spiritual and Biblical flavor, rueful songs about drinking too much, rhythm and blues and soul and pop and folk and bluegrass songs, and the first of several songs he would write concerning Australia's aborigines, "Maralinga," about British atomic testing in South Australia's native lands. *Gossip* also brought him to America for the first time: A&M Records released a fifteen-song version of the record in the United States, and Kelly and the band—now called the Messengers ("the name Coloured Girls, a joke that stuck, had caused confusion and offense") toured the States by bus, playing small clubs and theaters.

Back in Australia they made *Under the Sun* (1987), *So Much Water So Close to Home* (1989), and *Comedy* (1991), which featured another song about aboriginal politics, "From Little Things Big Things Grow," co-written with aboriginal songwriter Kev Carmody and detailing the land struggles of the Gurindji people in Australia's Northern Territory.

Then, with sadness but conviction, Kelly broke up the Messengers. His explanation is simple: "We were too good at what we were doing. It wasn't hard enough anymore. We had forged a style together but if we had kept going it would have gotten formulaic and that's why I ended it. I wanted to try and start moving into other areas, start mixing things up." The band's last record was released posthumously, so to speak: *Hidden Things,* a collection of B-sides and unreleased songs from various recording sessions.

\* \* \*

So began the startlingly eclectic and adventurous Modern Paul Kelly Era, in which the aimless young man so very proud of his four-line train song at age twenty nears the age of fifty as a polymath who has been an actor in films and on stage (starting as a gas-station attendant in a play in Adelaide and most recently playing the leading man in the film *One Night the Moon*), composed and performed music for plays, written songs with and for many other musicians and singers, produced a dozen records for other singers and bands, composed and performed music for films (most recently the hit movie *Lantana*), published a book of his lyrics ("passionate, direct, and forceful" poetry, according to the Melbourne daily newspaper, *The Age*), issued a hugely popular greatest-hits record, toured alone and with other musicians in North America, Europe, and Australia, made a "dub-reggae funk" record with the Australian band Professor Ratbaggy, made a wry and gentle bluegrass record (*Smoke*) with the Australian bluegrass band Uncle Bill, released six new rock and pop records of his own with a new band, remarried, lived in Los Angeles briefly, fathered two new sisters for his son, and in general pursued his musical and writing itch to whatever hemisphere or genre it led him.

The new band, the band he's been with since 1995, is made of Melbourne men: Spencer Jones and Shane O'Mara on guitars, Bruce Haymes on piano and organ, Steve Hadley on bass, and Peter Luscombe on drums. "We never have quite settled on a name for the band," says Kelly. "Got a good one?"

"I keep suggesting the Peter Luscombe Band but no one'll go for it," says Luscombe, a burly cheerful man who lived briefly in Pittsburgh as a child and vividly remembers watching "gloriously silly" American television shows filled with shoe telephones and space robots and disappearing genies with bare midriffs.

With this group, Kelly made *Deeper Water* (1995), *Live at the Continental and the Esplanade,* (1996), *Words and Music* (1998), and *Nothing But a Dream* (2001), this last as close to a solo project as anything he's recorded since *Post* in 1985; all of the songs except the roaring "Love Is The Law" are lean gentle ballads with Kelly on guitar and piano and only a guest or two accompanying him. "A record I've wanted to make for ten years, and saved songs for," he says. "Simple songs, a cycle of love and loss and love and memory and love. The songs rise up to 'Love Is The Law' in the middle and then slide gently away to the end. I thought a lot about the arrangement and pacing of songs on that record. You want to tell a story. I wanted it to be a journey."

\* \* \*

Most of Kelly's songs begin in his kitchen, or in the little shed he has in his back yard in Saint Kilda, a beachfront neighborhood of Melbourne. "Most of my ideas come from noodling around with the guitar on my own or with a friend or two in the kitchen," he says.

"For me, it's the music first. No one's going to listen to the words unless the music is interesting in some way. Sometimes a lyric will grow out of me just singing phrasing over chords. No words at that point, just humming, maybe a couple of phrases. Words are the aftertaste. I hear scraps of music all the time in my head and I try to catch those, to get down the lines of melody, and then once I start playing around with an idea I'll hum it and play it into a tape recorder. The lyrics at that point are a kind of mumbling, a proto-language. I'm singing sounds. Words are just something later for the sake of making sense from those first sounds. I think of lyrics as a fall from grace, a falling from the dream state of making a song into the waking state, the bolder step, of finishing a song."

> But I fell in love with whispers
> And I turned them into songs

Songwriting is essentially "serious fun," he says. "You never know how it's going to happen. It's coming from you but it's happening to you as well. It's similar to religious feelings. A religious impulse or awareness is about feeling connected to something larger than yourself. That's what happens when you manage to catch a song—you feel blessed. You feel suddenly connected. Maybe writing songs is like fishing—it's play, it's aimless. It's just fooling around, just taking pleasure in riffing on some chords, doodling, and if you're lucky, you get a bite on the line.

"Of course it then gives rise to all those other things like arranging songs, recording them, playing them, rehearsing them, trying to sell records, and all that is like any other job, there are things you have to do, to achieve, you have to be at your soundcheck by five o'clock, your concerts by eight. But the thing that gives rise to all this is just play. And play abetted by a band, by bandmates you trust. You want to be comfortable with your friends and get to a sort of ensemble ethos. Filmmakers and theatrical directors and producers use the same crews and teams for their work, and I think bands are like that—you trust people who have worked with you to make leaps with you.

"You develop shortcuts, you develop your own inner language as a band, a non-verbal language that lets you make leaps without plotting every step of the way. At the same time you want a certain difficulty in the band, strong opinions, eclectic tastes, lots of influences on the music, the ability to fight creatively. You don't want to get too facile."

* * *

Songs come to Kelly from everywhere and everything. Words spoken at the funeral of an elderly friend sparked a song called "The Pretty Place." The reckless drinking and drug-taking of another friend sparked the exuberant song "Careless." A request for a holiday song, from a festival in Adelaide, led to the most unusual Christmas song "Making Gravy," in which a prisoner writes a piercing letter to his brother, visualizing the roast turkey dinner and subsequent dancing at the family homestead, worrying about his wife and children, begging his brother not to dance too close to the prisoner's wife, and promising to make the gravy himself when he's free, as amends for his sins. A Raymond Carver short story led to one of Kelly's most-requested songs, "Everything's Turning to White," about a murder and the fading of love. The Australian touchstone story of Vincent Lingari, the Aboriginal leader who inspired his people's eight-year peaceful battle to reclaim their land, led to "From Little Things Big Things Grow." The life of Australian cricket legend the late Sir Donald Bradman, the greatest player ever in his sport and the hero of Australia's 1930 thrashing of the imperial English team, led to the song "Bradman," also much-requested (especially in Scandinavia, for some reason, reports Kelly).

Talk of that song makes him grin: "I sent a copy of the song and the video to Sir Don himself, who'd retired back to Adelaide, with a letter noting that he'd known my dad John. The Don—the greatest sporting legend in Australian history—was famous for writing responses to fans by hand, and sure enough I got a hand-written note one day. 'Thank you for your attempt,' he wrote, and then pointed out that maybe pop musicians had the money for videotape players but *he* certainly didn't."

There are also many rueful Paul Kelly songs about drinking: "Little Decisions," about not making the big promises that are so easy to break; "Stories of Me," about listening bitterly to friends' endless humiliating stories of your bottom-of-the-glass days; "I Don't Remember a Thing," which is about not remembering a thing. And there are many dozens of Kelly songs about love and lust, some of them biting and hilarious, like the one which drolly and profanely accounts the travels of a yearning man following a fleeting girlfriend through Europe, but many of them also piercingly honest about the million intricate joys and pains of love. For example, "If I Could Start Today Again":

I only want one day
To unsay the things I said
Undo the thing I did
One lousy day that's all
Of every day that's been before
Since time began

And even Kelly, not a man given to introspective analysis of his work, has noticed that many of the songs he's written in his forties are considerations of time and entropy, of sweet past moments savored in memory, of love not so much youthfully headlong and careless now but deeper, more graceful, brave under inevitable duress. "I'm always aware of time passing," he says. "I've always been aware that a large part of living is losing things. I have a terrible memory, so life to me always feels like it's slipping away. Maybe making music is like putting out a net so that something is there, at least—so you have something in your hands, if only a trace. Maybe if you're aware of death coming, then life becomes stronger-tasting."

Yes, I wasted time
Now time is wasting me
Soon it's closing time
Won't you stay with me?

Molly took my hand and led the way
Now Molly's yellow hair has turned to gray
She wore a red dress she let me undo
Though Molly swears that day her dress was blue

"I'm just fascinated by songs," says Kelly. "I've always wanted to just make them. I wasn't interested in telling my story, or confessing things, or expressing myself, or writing as therapy. There were songs I heard on the radio as a kid that just arrested me, they seemed so magical—and I wanted to try to make those things too. I wanted to put words to music. It's very simple, but utterly mysterious."

Kelly's book of poems, *Lyrics*, opens with a telling quote, from Anton Chekhov: "I don't have what you would call a philosophy or coherent world view so I shall have to limit myself to describing how my heroes love, marry, give birth, die, and speak."

"I have people come up to me all the time and say 'how did you know my story? That song—it's about me!'" says Kelly. "I've felt like that about other people's songs. I've felt their power, and I wanted to take hold of that power myself. Making songs is like sending out little arrows, and you'll never really know where your arrows land."

I was standing in the schoolyard
I guess it was sometime in 1965
Just me and my friends listening to the radio
And a song came on called "I Feel Fine"
The playground sounds grew dim
The whole wide world seemed to fade
There was nothing but me
And that heavenly sound
Burning in my brain:
Words and music.

\* \* \*

Kelly and his band opened their 2002 tour of North America in Seattle, at the Crocodile Café. The stage was the size of a table and there were no seats for the audience and the room was so cold you could see your breath. The floor was sticky and the sweet-faced waitress had bright pink hair. There was an earnest and passionate warm-up band, a trio recruited at the last minute when the scheduled act canceled, and after they finished with a wild flourish of guitars and looked at each other with mingled delight and relief (we *did* it!) there followed a few quiet moments during which scratchy Delta blues songs filled the sound system (songs, it turns out, from Kelly's own disc collection, which he carries with him in a worn case) and then Paul walked quietly into the spotlight alone and began to sing "Just About to Break":

I'm gonna rock your head
Start a burning in your bed

Then he sang the lean prayer "If I Could Start Today Again" and then without fanfare the band wandered casually onstage, carefully stepping over wires and speakers, and they spent the next two hours displaying the full range of Paul Kelly songs: musing ballads, howling rockers, wild rave-ups, spirituals, drinking songs, rhythm and blues and soul and pop and folk. They played "Love Is The Law" so loud that beer bottles rattled on the back bar. They played "To Her Door," the crowd singing along as a forlorn and recently sober man and his loving but cautious wife meet again in the song after a year apart, their children watching nervously. They played a shimmering version of "Midnight Rain" in which the narrator wonders where his former lover is now and if it's raining there and if she's barefoot and if she's alone. They played the bitter rant "Little Kings," one of the rare songs on which Kelly drops his songwriting mask and speaks acidly about Australian politics:

In the land of the little kings
Profit is the only thing
And everywhere the little kings
Are getting away with murder
In the land of the little kings
Justice don't mean a thing

And they played Paul's song for his mother and father, and "Winter Coat," a song he wrote on a cold day in an Australian town called Sunshine, and the headlong exuberant grateful prayer "Careless," and ten other songs, and near the end they played a song that's maybe the most epic and telling and complex of all the hundreds of songs Paul Kelly has written. It's called "Deeper Water," and it begins with a boy on the beach walking with his father, and his father's hand is strong and sure, and the boy grows up and dives into the deeper water of lust and then love, and one night he feels his child inside his wife and his waters grow deeper, and then years later his wife sickens to the bone and fades into the deepest water of all, and the song ends with the bereaved man taking his small son to the beach, and every time I hear that song I end up weeping and thinking of the incredible intricate endless riveting layers and layers and layers of human love and loss and joy. Which is what Paul Kelly catches so often in the stories he begins in his kitchen, humming in the late afternoon, fishing with his guitar for a song that was never ever in the world before.

\* \* \*

Every Wednesday afternoon at five o'clock, just as the afternoon is leaning into evening, fifteen or so men gather in a park in Saint Kilda, the waterfront neighborhood of the city of Melbourne. The men are of various ages from their twenties to their late forties. Most are musicians and writers and comedians and actors and such. They carry shoes with studs that grip grassy fields, and several carry an Australian-rules football, a cross between an American football and a rugby ball. When they arrive in the park they chaff and banter in the way of all men everywhere engaged in any work or play or war with other men. They lounge on the grass and stretch and groan and complain about their sore knees and tell funny stories and exchange news and gossip and inquire about wives and girlfriends and children. Then slowly they form themselves into a ragged circle and they begin to run, first slowly, jogging and milling their arms to get their shoulders loose, and then some run faster, but others stay at the original loose pace, so that after a few minutes all the men are moving in a large counterclockwise circle at a pace comfortable to each. They move in groups of three or four, kicking and punching (or "hand-passing," as they say) the ball to each other. He who receives the ball is instantly the center of the ever-changing formation, as the other three fan out from him and call for the ball; when he kicks or passes it to a colleague, the new receiver is then the new center-spoke from whom the others fan out, their voices ringing in the broad late afternoon light.

This is called "circle work" in Australia, and it is the traditional pre-lude and warm-up to a game of Australian-rules football, or footy, the national sport. In this case, however, the circle work *is* the game, and for one of the players at least the Wednesday evening ragged grinning panting circle of men is meditation and exercise and art form and nostalgia and club and tribe and team and band and sweet sweaty prayer. "It's my church, and bliss, and prayer," says Kelly. "That's where I focus and relax and slip away into the motions of the game. An old game, a lovely game, born in Melbourne in 1858, in what was then a horse paddock. Based partly on rugby and partly on an ancient aboriginal game. British and Aboriginal, colonial and original. I went to my first game when I was seven years old—the Norwood Redlegs, in Adelaide. I've been hooked ever since."

The park on Saint Kilda Street where they play is large, more than two hundred meters long, and the circle work might last ninety minutes or so. "You smell the cut grass, and liniment, and dubbin—the lard you rub on the ball to waterproof it," says Paul. "You hear the banter and encouragement and traffic in the distance. No one's in charge and no one calls the time. We just play until we stop. You hear the dull thwack of feet and hands hitting balls. Guys tire and peel away but there's always one or two groups that keep going. That's a sweet time, kicking as the light begins to fail. Time slows down and you're back in your childhood, playing ball with your mates until the last drop of light. You half expect your mum to call you in for dinner."

Sometimes the men playing football in the park on Saint Kilda Street will flop down in the grass at dusk and share a beer, but "that's only on ceremonial occasions, like musicians leaving for tours or someone marrying," says Kelly. At the end of the season, in December, they have a competitive and hilarious "superkick," a contest measuring accuracy, distance, and style ("style meaning how mongrelly your kicks are"), but that's generally the extent of formal ceremony, a fact Kelly savors.

It's the loose flow he loves: the endless creativity of it, the moving through the fading light, the blending of sounds and voices into a dappled liquid moment that is both immanent and immediately past at once, physical and emotional, intense and relaxed, shared and solitary, sweet and piercing, rough and skilled, passionate and smooth, careful and careless, raw and holy.

# CHAPTER ELEVEN

# A Sturdy Man

I met Bob Boehmer when he was seventy-eight years old and I was thirty-four. He was a short tough man with a chest like a refrigerator and a perfectly round belly that hung between his suspenders like a face between fenceposts. His face was the color and consistency of bark and his nose had a neat left turn in it near its point. His ears had been mashed by cleats and fists long ago and they looked like tulip petals. His jaw looked like the business end of an axe. He spoke beautifully in a halting woodsy drawl and he used an endless cascade of interesting words. I never once heard him curse or raise his voice. When he was annoyed he would raise his eyebrows, which looked like caterpillars.

His wife was the quietest woman I ever met and their three sons were quieter. Bob was quiet, too. He was the first of six children, and lived to see his one sister and four brothers dead, Philip Kenneth Lois Barney and Johnny, Phil in a factory accident and the rest eaten by cancers. It must have broken his heart to see his brothers and sister and parents die, one after another, leaving him an elderly orphan, but he rarely spoke of this sadness, for he was a discreet man, loath to burden you with information you did not want, although no man enjoyed the trivial and esoteric as much as Bob, and no man so cherished discovering the etiology of things: buildings, names, towns, businesses, customs. He loved wandering through the University of Portland's voluminous dank archives in this characteristic pursuit of the small but telling detail. He also loved chaffing the archives' elderly keepers, for he was older than they were and no respecter of age as privilege.

He told tales with energy and affection and burnished skill. Stories of the two boyhood years he lived in a tent on Portland Boulevard, on a lot thick with fir trees, while his father built a house for the family—a house later flattened by the State of Oregon and replaced with the southbound lane of Interstate Highway 5. Stories about being left back in sixth grade at Holy Redeemer School because very often instead of walking to school he walked to a golf course where he could make sixty cents for caddying all day. Stories about the wet afternoons he spent on the corner of Albina and Killingsworth Streets in Portland, hawking copies of the *News,* the *Telegram,* the *Journal,* and the *Oregonian.* Stories about dragging a wagon through the rain with copies of *The Country Gentleman* and *The Saturday Evening Post* and *Liberty* for sale. Stories about the summers he spent wandering Oregon as a teenager at work in the far fields, "jigging sacks of wheat, baling hay, picking prunes, picking apples, fending off the working girls who came to visit the hay-balers when we flopped down in the flophouses," as he said. Stories about his father George, a printer's devil in Aberdeen, South Dakota, who played cornet in the South Dakota State Band, who arrived in Portland in 1911 with eleven dollars in his pocket. Stories about his grandfather Andrew, who died mysteriously in Cheyenne County, Minnesota, shot in the temple, whether by his own hand or someone else's no one ever knew. Stories about his (Bob's) roustabout days in the United States Army Air Corps, and how he was named commander of the Southern Pacific troop train taking recruits from Portland to the Presidio in San Francisco for processing, and lost eleven recruits in bars along the way, and how when he marched for the first time in formation at a base in Texas he marched one way and the rest of the company marched the other and the drill instructor's voice "burned the hair right off the side of my head," and stories of how Technical Sergeant Boomer Boehmer got in a bar brawl in North Africa during the war, and (he would say with a sloooooooow wink) woke up with a new tattoo of a rose on his left buttock.

"I don't believe it, Robert," I'd say.

"Want to see it?" he'd ask, reaching for his belt.

Stories about the time he accidentally shot himself in the hand with a Belgian pistol in Africa during the war, the bullet passing completely through his hand, puncturing the mosquito netting around his bed, and ending up in a wallet in the back pocket of a soldier walking by. Stories of his other war days in Malta (where he was on loan to England's Royal Air Force), Sardinia, Sicily, Germany. Stories about his days as a lumbermen's representative in the State of Washington, in which capacity he got to know every knockabout sawmill and gyppo outfit in the woods of the Pacific Northwest, wandering his vast territory ("from the crest of the Cascades to the sea, from Chehalis to British Columbia") with his golf clubs in his trunk, with a well-thumbed United States Geological Survey map on the seat beside him, with his tweed hat perched on his crewcut head, his crewcut like a fresh-mown lawn, a song on his lips, a notebook in his pocket.

"I knew damned near every lumberman in the West—maybe *every* one, come to think of it," he told me once, in the course of a story about how he learned to spot hookers and card-sharps at the annual lumbermen's convention at the St. Francis Hotel in San Francisco—a convention at which Bob didn't take a drop of his favorite concoction, Scotch and water, because he was running the convention and needed to be "attuned," as he said.

"How could you tell the sharps?" I asked.

"By the way they dressed."

"How could you tell the hookers?"

"You just . . . could," he said. "They had a certain self-assurance."

Stories of his days as a Columbia University boy in 1934, playing football, boxing in Monogram Club "smokers" in Howard Hall in 1935 (he lost), running for junior class president in 1936 (he won), reporting for *The Columbiad* (predecessor to *The Beacon*), stories about how he ran out of money and couldn't graduate with his class in 1937 and ended up working deep in the woods in Idaho building dams with the Army Corps of Engineers (he finished his degree in 1947, the year he won *The Beacon* student newspaper contest for best short story written by an undergraduate, with a story called "Winter Rain," a short, hard, eloquent piece of work about an Italian father who resolves to murder the American soldier who impregnated and abandoned his daughter), stories of his days as a reporter in California, where he lived across the hall from an apartmentful of stewardesses, stories of his brief career as a counterman in a camera store, this brief career enlivened by the day that John Steinbeck came in to get his camera fixed and Bob, knowing he was in the presence of a master storyteller, was speechless; stories of his days as a writer and editor on the *McMinnville Telephone-Register* and *The Oregon Journal,* which latter sent ace reporter Bob Boehmer on the first commercial 707 flight from New York to Paris, where Bob spent three days at the Follies, finally filing a single brief story (not about the Follies).

"You know, they never sent me anywhere ever again," he said wonderingly.

Tales of his adventures and misadventures as, variously, the University of Portland's news bureau director, editor of the *Alumni*

*Bulletin,* placement officer, *Log* advisor, alumni association secretary, acting public relations director, *Portland Magazine* writer (articles by him about boxing, typefaces, the Vanport flood, track, the Class of 1936, the Tillamook Burn, and football appeared there, and no man ever contributed more class notes, although in his later years those notes were increasingly accounts of funerals, each carefully typed with appended lists of the other alumni he had noticed at the wake, church, cemetery), and general editor-of-all-trades in the public relations office from 1947 to 1951 and then again from 1978 until he died. Tales of his little cabin at Arch Cape, on the Oregon coast, where he spent his summers cutting brush and reading and working his land and watching the sea. Stories and tales and anecdotes and jokes and poems and musings and memories. It was by his tales that I came to learn what poet Wendell Berry calls "the order of his delight," and it is by his tales that I will remember the sturdy little man.

He read widely and well and his sterling mind never stopped ranging far afield. One fall day I innocently asked him what he had read that summer at his Arch Cape cabin.

"The complete works of F. Scott Fitzgerald; *Messer Marco Polo* by Donn Byrne; a history of Oregon coastal trails; *Poor People* by Fyodor Dostoevsky; a history of the Tillamook Burn; and something by Stewart Holbrook that wasn't all that great, I'm sorry to say, for I like Holbrook, a terrific storyteller. Did you ever read Holbrook's *The Far Corner* . . ." and he was off and running on a story that started with the fact that Holbrook was a Vermonter by birth and came west first to work as a logger in the jungles of British Columbia before nailing his Boston derby hat to a stump in the deep cedar woods and taking a train to Portland, and then touched on the fact that he and Holbrook had many mutual friends (among them Ellis Lucia and Walt Mattilla and a really startling number of newspaper, public relations, or literary men like Bob Mahaffey, Dave James, Bill Hagenstein, Don Holm, and James Stevens), and slid sideways into accounts of such legendary woodsfolk as the logger Jigger Jones, who could walk a felled spruce barefoot and kick off every knot, and who coined the famous logger battle-cry *I can run faster, jump higher, and spit further than any son-of-a-bitch in this camp!;* and the shanghai crimp Bunco Kelly, who usually sold drunken loggers (for fifty dollars) to ships bound for the Far East but who once sold a wooden Indian to a British ship, which pitched it overboard near the mouth of the Columbia, from which rich waters it was fished by astonished Finnish salmon fishermen; and the great logging-camp brawler Silver Jack Driscoll, who could fell an ox with one punch; and ended up being about Erickson's Saloon, a Portland emporium legendary among loggers and sailors and journalists and much mourned by Holbrook, who had been a steady customer until the day he started seeing bats and winged eels where there weren't any, and so retired from the drinking life.

Erickson's didn't *close*, exactly, said Bob; it shrank, in a most unsaloonlike fashion. Once it was a block long, with five entrances on various streets, and a bouncer at each door, but then it began to close a door here and there, and pieces of the saloon were sold off, and then finally it was a little hole in the wall, and then one day it just wasn't there anymore.

\* \* \*

Here are some other things to know about Bob:

He never forgot anything and never misplaced a sheet of paper.

He wrote all editorial comments in pencil.

He carried his mother's rosary in his left-hand pants pocket.

He wiped his glasses clean using the fat end of his tie.

He disliked using the phone to do a task his legs would carry him to.

He called heavy editing of a manuscript a "rewrite," which is what it is.

He perched his glasses on his crewcut when musing.

He seemed naive but he was not.

He had a habit of crooking his finger at me and saying, sonorously, "I would have words with you"—a courteous locution.

He never stopped using his typewriter, because, he said, the sound was workmanlike, although when electronic mail suddenly became normal in 1994 or so Bob easily got into the habit of it. His first e-mail message was to his second son.

He could identify, by sight and touch and sometimes by taste, some one hundred species of trees, and perhaps twice that many species of bushes and plants.

He knew where elk slept in his woods at Arch Cape, and did not scythe the grassy beds they came back to every winter, but let them grow, "so there's spring in their mattress."

He had exactly four-tenths of an acre of woods, he said, and I believe he knew every tree on his four-tenths of an acre of woods. A woods had to be worked, he said, or else the idea of owning it was irresponsible, and so he cut brush and vines and poison oak, and kept walking trails clear, and carted firewood to his cabin, and planted trees, and weeded the flowers his wife set out at the feet of the firs, and cut what little lawn there was, until there came a time that he could not cut and weed and cart and plant, which greatly saddened him, and much reduced his joy at being in his cabin, a joy that had been patent.

He knew what fish were running at what time of the year off Arch Cape, and when I asked him how he knew this he told me that he kept a weather eye on the gear of the fishing boats. Once when he was looking out to sea he saw a bald eagle, the only one he ever saw at the Cape. I did not tell him then that I thought he looked like a bald eagle himself: close-cropped white head, prominent beak, sharp eye, a predilection for fish.

He once showed me a spruce tree in which he had seen a black bear sleeping. He stared at the tree with real reverence; it had held the king of the woods, if only for a night ("a bear could kick a cougar all to pieces, you know"), and Bob ever after felt a special affection for that tree, refusing to cut it even when it died.

He showed me another tree in which he had seen a great gray owl as big as a child.

He once handed me a tiny Douglas fir and told me to plant it in my yard, and told me that when it was three feet tall I would be a real Oregonian, having nursed a tree. The tree is now taller than my daughter. It reminds me of Bob.

He knew that cottonwood made the loveliest plywood, and that plywood had been invented not far from the University, by the Portland Manufacturing Company, in Portland's St. Johns neighborhood. He knew how to leach red dye from sawn alder. He knew that alder trees often curved together in canopies over streambeds and that alder of that sort would dry crookedly, in the shape of its original bend, and that this was called tension alder, and that it was the bane of sawmills. He knew what species of trees would snap first when overburdened with wet snow or thick ice: elm, birch, white maple.

At his city home in North Portland, a mile from where he was born, two miles from the University, he and his wife had a lush tiny garden in which there were beans, begonias, carrots, claredendrons, dahlias, figs, firs, garlic, grapes, irises, lanaria, marigolds, myrtle, onions, pears, peas, plums, potatoes, radishes, raspberries, rhododendrons, roses, sedums, snapdragons, squashes, strawberries, thyme, violets, zinnias, and an apple tree which Bob had pruned in such a way that it grew horizontally along the porch from west to east like a long green arm.

Once I walked into his garden with him and walked out a few minutes later with garlic and radishes filling my pockets. Also in my pockets were sprigs of thyme, which dried and became powder that made my ancient raincoat a redolent thing. Recently I reached into a pocket and my fingers came away covered with thyme dust, which smells loud and reminds me of Bob.

He founded the Waud's Bluff Literary & Jawing Society, which consisted initially of two members, him and me, and which demanded of its members the recitation of a poem from memory before lunch, which was always at Dan and Louis' Oyster Bar on Ankeny Street in Portland, Oregon. Although he once recited all forty-four lines of Henry Wadsworth Longfellow's "The Day Is Done" from memory, more often he would recite limericks before slurping Garibaldi crab stew and sipping buttermilk, which was forbidden by his doctor and his wife, and which the waitress brought without asking. Bob always wrapped his buttermilk in a napkin in case his doctor or his wife or both should suddenly appear in Dan and Louis' Oyster Bar. "God forbid such a thing, although I like the man and love the woman," he would say.

Once he said, "I have a joke about Vassar girls."

"Robert, are you about to tell me a dirty joke?"

"Yes."

"Okay."

"If all the Vassar girls in the world were laid end to end (long pause), I wouldn't be surprised."

This was the only vaguely dirty joke he ever told me.

He once spent a whole Waud's Bluff Literary & Jawing Society meeting telling me how he met his wife, Gabrielle. He was the University's alumni relations director at the time and she was a professor of nursing. A caravan of cars and people from the University was heading to eastern Oregon on an admissions recruiting trip. Gabrielle, a native of Baker (now Baker City) in that dry part of the state, was to go along. She'd been told to meet the caravan on a streetcorner but the message was garbled and she waited in a hotel lobby.

"So I was mad at her before I became mad for her," said Bob. "Our first date was at the Guild Theater. We went to see the movie *Gigi*, with Leslie Caron and Gene Kelly. Very good movie."

"Did you kiss her?"

"No."

He once walked into my office and showed me the diary his mother kept in 1913, the year he was born. Here is the first entry: "Born: our first child, a boy. May God bless our boy and help us to guide and guard it." The handwriting is that of his father, who wrote entries for two weeks in a sudden slanting hand until his wife returned home with "the Boy" and resumed her writing. Her handwriting was quiet and circular. (Bob's father never did name his son in the diary; after carefully noting his son's intermittent feeding habits for two weeks, he ends his entries with "Louise and the Boy came home today. The Boy is trying to be real good.")

Another day he walked into my office with another diary, this one his own from his years in the Army. It was more of a daybook, or scrapbook, than a diary, really, as it contained snippets of newspaper articles, witticisms read and overheard, lists ("Fifteen Hints on Marriage," "Eight Rules for Failure," a survey of cattle brands), poems, the definitions of interesting words, books to read, films seen, cartoons he liked, travelogues of towns he was stationed in or passing through. In his lovely handwriting there is a note from a trip to Rome in 1944: ". . . a drinkfest at the club—*remember* how when each man would complete his tale another would say, 'Now let me tell *my* story.' . . ."

Often he would walk into my office with a snippet of poetry very nearly lost to the world but not to Bob. Once, after we'd spoken of wars and the dead too young, he walked into my office and handed me this shred of the poem "For the Fallen," by Laurence Binyon (1869–1943):

> They shall not grow old,
> As we that are left grow old;
> Age shall not weary them
> Nor the years condemn.
> At the going down of the sun
> And in the morning
> We shall remember them.

\* \* \*

As a football player, Bob was small and tough—a "watch-charm guard," in the lovely old phrase so beloved of sportswriter Grantland Rice. A friend of his from his college football days told me this story, which Bob swore was a lie, but the storyteller was Edward O'Meara, "and I am a professional newspaperman and so have never told a lie," as Ed said. One day the Columbia University freshmen were scrimmaging the Columbia Prep School varsity. There was only a year in age between the two squads, but there was that gaping social chasm between high school and college, and so the scrimmage was ferocious, with a great many fouls and stealthy punches. After one angry pileup the teams trudged back to their huddles. One college player remained at the scrimmage line, a small sturdy fellow who tore off his helmet, faced the Prep boys, cocked his fists, and said, grimly, "I'll fight you one at a time, or I'll fight you all at once!"

This was Bob.

Another friend of Bob's, Henry Eder, told me another football story about Bob. In 1933 Henry and Bob were the pulling guards on the freshman football team; one play called for them both to pull to the right to lead the blocking for a sweep; Henry pulled right; Bob pulled left; the resulting headlong collision left them huddled together in a heap. "The resultant loss of brainpower led him to be an editor in later life," said Henry.

"That's a lie, too," said Bob. "Although I did become an editor."

Bob was a "photogrammatrist," his word, during the Second World War, a man who specialized in photo reconnaissance—reading the photographs taken by pilots, analyzing them for ammunition dumps, culverts, roads, camps. He and his colleagues also made the photos into maps used to orient bomber pilots to the terrain they'd bomb. Bob was proud that his maps indirectly saved much of Rome from being razed. When the war ended he took a crowded troop ship to New York City and then instantly boarded a crowded troop train and rode all day and night for three days to Portland, where he got off the train at Union Station and walked home, several miles.

Over the years Bob had been "edited heavily by surgeons," as he said, and he'd lost a gallbladder and two testicles (at age eighty-one—"well, shoot, no more sons," he said ruefully) and several lumps and cysts and melanomas of various sizes, and had a triple bypass heart operation, the result of a heart attack suffered one day as he walked into his office on the fourth floor of Waldschmidt Hall. He pitched forward on his face just after he crossed under the lintel. He was taken down the stairs on a stretcher and rushed to the hospital. He had no recollection of all this, which he regretted, for he said many times that he would have enjoyed being carried down those damned stairs, since he had damn well labored up them so damned many times. Partly as a memorial to this red-letter day and partly as a precaution he carried with him a Heart Valve Patient Identification card from American Edwards Laboratories in Santa Ana, California. The card noted that George Boehmer had had a prosthetic heart valve, size 10A, implanted on October 29, 1985. It also noted the serial number, AV8718, and the model number, 1260, of the valve: "so Gabrielle can send it back for a refund after I kick the bucket, I guess," he said one day.

His health was extraordinary for a man of eighty-four years but he had to take various pills of various colors for various ailments and the pills made his handwriting a fragile thing. He used a typewriter whenever possible because his shaky scrawl embarrassed him. Once he presented me with a book by Stewart Holbrook (*The Wonderful West*, not one of Holbrook's best) and I asked him to sign it. Writing his signature took him nearly two minutes, and as I watched his hand crawl slowly across the page I was ashamed of my thoughtlessness.

He was a bibliophile of the first water and no man ever took more delight in finding an extraordinarily beautiful book for fifty cents. In the end he favored content over form but it was a near thing. More than once I saw him buy a book simply for its beauty as a printed object; he once bought a *Liturgy of the Hours* (for fifty cents) because it was bound in a novel fashion, and I have before me a copy of Henry Van Dyke's *The Man Behind the Book* (1929), which he presented to me as a fine example of a "foiled" cover, as he said. (I also have before me Bob's foiled-cover edition of *Garrulities of an Octogenarian Editor* [1923], by Henry Holt, which makes me smile.) He was a past master of the exotica of bindings, glue, papers, inks, imprints, frontispieces, tissue sheets, stitching, dingbats, doohickeys, and bookplates. He was also a serious scholar of prefaces, afterwords, notes on the type, notes on the author, and the other ephemera of bookish prose, and the sort of man who could use printer's words like *deckle, em, en, intaglio,* and *quoin* and expect you to know them, and the sort of man who knew offhandedly that the notation "-30-" at the end of a manuscript had come originally from telegraph operators, who used it as a sign-off because it was easy to stroke. Also he had a hawk eye for detail work on drop-cap lettering and the art that once led chapter heads in books. It was his considered opinion that the finest practitioner of this sort of thing, at least in the Pacific Northwest, was the legendary Oregon printer and writer Ben Hur Lampman (who received an honorary doctorate from the University at Bob's eventual graduation ceremony, in 1947), and it is a reflection of Bob's omnivorous and gleeful bookishness that I once saw him buy (again for fifty cents) a copy of Lampman's *How Could I Be Forgetting*, a book that I knew Bob had. In fact I knew he had several copies of it.

"*Another* one?" I asked.

"Lord, son, look at the beautiful binding," he said.

He walked around the campus once a day if the weather was clear. He walked very slowly, "so as not to tax the ticker." This pace allowed him to talk, which he did, beautifully.

He and I spent many hours together, poring over the proof sheets and galleys and bluelines of various publications, looking for small errors, telling stories. Thousands of hours, thousands of stories. He savored stories and told them beautifully. He had a special affection for the peccadillos of the University's faculty and staff, and he remembered a truly startling number of, as he said, "whiskey priests, amorous secretaries, dignified thieves, fools and mountebanks and charlatans of all sorts and styles." He treasured tales of misadventure and told them with such gentle amusement and wry identification that they became not gossip at all but the rueful accounting of human foolishness and so a sort of prayer for all fools, which is to say all of us.

He had a great horror of interrupting a colleague during concentration and so would often stand quietly in an office door, holding a sheet of paper, his pencil cocked behind his ear, waiting. I have seen him wait in this fashion for more than five minutes. This is how I remember him best. All the rest of my life as I am working and writing and reading and playing with my daughter and sons I will pretend that Bob is standing behind me, his belly peeking out between his suspenders, his pencil jutting up from his ear like a yellow horn, his glasses perched atop the lawn of his hair, his features composed in his old man zen face, a sheet of yellow legal paper in his hand, his careful crabbed handwriting visible on the paper. His peace is as big as the ocean. He is waiting to see me.

Now I am waiting to see him.

CHAPTER ONE
Van Morrison

O, where to start talking about the great musical genius of our time . . . well, if you have not heard much Van, I direct you to The Six Holy Records in a Row, which is to say:

*No Guru, No Method, No Teacher* (1986)
*Poetic Champions Compose* (1987)
*Irish Heartbeat* (1988)
*Avalon Sunset* (1989)
*Enlightenment* (1990)
*Hymns to the Silence* (1991)

And then you can poke around freely in The Canon. Do listen to *Astral Weeks,* preferably with your lover in the evening by the fire with a bottle of excellent red wine and no particular place to go, and for a taste of the best wild mad chanting exuberant testy terrific Van live in concert I recommend the 1994 double record *A Night in San Francisco.* By then, after nine Van records, you will either be a Van fan for life or utterly sick of the Man's quest for rapture. I bet the former.

There are about twenty million things published about Van, almost all of them thin soup and shallow sea. The best book is Brian Hinton's *Celtic Crossroads: The Art of Van Morrison* (Unwin Brothers, 1997), which is thorough, detailed, historically minded, not fan fawn, not apologia, and gracefully written. It also contains a terrific discography and an oceanic index of Van detail at the end. A heroic job of scholarship about the greatest Irish poet since Yeats, all due respect to Seamus Heaney and Nuala ni Dhomhnaill.

There are also about eleven million Van websites, but the best of them, to my mind, is http://www.harbour.sfu.ca/~hayward/van/— sort of the official keeping-track-of-Van-stuff site. Another heroic labor of love, of which there are, delightfully, so very many in this bruised & lovely world.


CHAPTER TWO
William Blake


Private Scolfield's last name is spelled variously Scofield, Scholfield, Schofield, and Scolfield, depending on what book you read. I have used the last spelling, Scolfield, for two reasons: first, it's a compromise nine letters between eight and ten, and second, it is the spelling used by James King in his book *William Blake: His Life* (St. Martin's Press, New York, 1991), and I regard King's book as the best single source of material on the trial. King also leans on two other fine sources, G. E. Bentley Jr. and Alexander Gilchrist, and so I lean toward King and his spelling as a matter of trust. Sometimes you just have to take a flyer on these things. Gilchrist's book, *Life of William Blake,* was first published in London in 1863.

Geoffrey Keynes is arguably the greatest Blake scholar of them all, and there have been plenty of glorious Blake nuts. Keynes's various books on Billy include *The Writings of William Blake, A Bibliography of William Blake,* and *The Letters of William Blake,* a beautiful and entertaining book. My edition of *The Letters* was published in 1956 by The Macmillan Company, New York.

David Erdman's *The Complete Poetry and Prose of William Blake* (University of California Press, 1982) is the best compendium of Blake's own work extant, in my opinion. Erdman, bless his soul, not only scoured through Billy's manuscripts and printed the pieces Blake struck out, but he also prints all Blake's scribblings in margins of books he was reading. Inasmuch as Billy was an inveterate scribbler, an impatient reader, and a man armed with a pencil at all times, this is a delightful window into the mind of the poet.

A superb selected Blake edition is *The Essential Blake,* edited and introduced by the poet Stanley Kunitz (The Ecco Press, New York, 1987). Kunitz, a hell of a poet himself, has chosen most of the very best Blake lyrics and fragments, and has included what he rightly calls the two absolutely basic Blake texts, *The Marriage of Heaven and Hell* and the *Songs of Innocence and of Experience.* The latter was also very beautifully set to music in 1986 by the American gravel-voiced folk genius Greg Brown. Trust me—once you hear his versions of Billy's songs, they will be in your mind for ever and ever amen.

Other books worthy of note, from which I have drawn material or corroborated same: *William Blake* by Osbert Burdett (New York, Macmillan, 1926); *William Blake* by Arthur Symons (Jonathan Cape, London, 1907); *The Human Face of God: William Blake and the Book of Job* by Kathleen Raine (Thames and Hudson, 1982); *William Blake: Painter, Poet, Visionary* by Kaethe Wolf-Gumpold (Rudolf Steiner Press, London, 1969), and *William Blake: The Politics of Vision* by Mark Schorer (Henry Holt & Co., New York, 1946). Commentators on Blake since his death in 1827 are legion, but a curious reader will dig up the commentaries of three extraordinary writers: William Butler Yeats, Charles Algernon Swinburne, and Peter Ackroyd. My favorite single biography of Billy is Mona Wilson's landmark *The Life of William Blake*, first published in 1927.

Trial details were checked with the legal scholar John Langbein, of Yale University Law School; with Dan Coquillette, of Boston College Law School; and with the estimable Professor G. E. Bentley, Jr., of the University of Toronto—one of the great Blake scholars ever, and probably the most eminent extant. His careful reading of my manuscript was a gift to me.

CHAPTER THREE
Plutarkos

As you might discern from the essay in this volume, the basic text for Plutarch is *The Lives,* but there are so very many of the Lives that he or she dipping a leery toe into the ocean of the greatest of the Greek essayists of character might start with a few of the best: Antony, Alexander, Cicero, Caesar, and Demosthenes. Plutarch is sort of like Van Morrison, in that a headlong plunge will leave you either addled with delight or sprinting in the other direction.

I also discovered, during my plunge into Plutarkos, that his work led me back to the great Latin writers Cicero and Livy; and then for some reason (I think Plutarch's long, looping sentences) into Gibbon. Whereupon I had to return to the Planet Earth or end up an assistant professor of something or other. God save us.

CHAPTER FOUR
## Robert Louis Stevenson

Many many people have written very well indeed of Stevenson, but the curious beginner ought to start with Ian Bell's lovely *Dreams of Exile,* the best of the modern books about Louis—J. C. Furnas's *Voyage to Windward* is the best of the older books, I think. Scholars sneer and pick like testy gulls at Graham Balfour's biography of his cousin, the first Stevenson biography ever written (except for all of Stevenson's work, which is essentially, as a whole, the autobiography of his imagination) but I loved it for its emotion and immediacy. It's called *The Life of Robert Louis Stevenson.* Ignore the scholars and read it if you can find a copy.

If, as I suspect is the case, you have not read Stevenson since you were a tadpole, I heartily recommend you hie yourself to the local bookstore and grab reasonably priced copies of *Treasure Island, Kidnapped,* and *Jekyll & Hyde,* and read them in that order, and then read the best collection of his essays (*The Lantern Bearers & Other Essays,* edited by Jeremy Treglown, published by Farrar Straus Giroux), and then if you are on an RLS tear, read *Travels with a Donkey* and *Weir of Hermiston,* which just ends in the middle of a sentence, very eerie. Sigh. What that man might have done further had he lived past age forty-four—but my, the wonderful things he did while alive. He lived hard and well, did Mr. Stevenson.

A last note: it's very interesting to me that many of the finest writers in the world are passionate Stevenson fans. For example, I think that Helen Garner is one of the finest Australian writers in the long colorful history of that colorful nation, and I met her recently, and as soon as we discovered we were both mad Stevensonians we were friends for life. And in these United States of America the maddest Stevenson fan of all is perhaps this country's finest writer, Cynthia Ozick.

I rest my case.


CHAPTER FIVE
## Rider Haggard

The basic Haggard texts, as you might suspect from my breezily opinionated essay, are *King Solomon's Mines* and *She.* But there are many, many pleasures in Haggard, and I find that once fairly begun into his works it's hard to stop, for reasons that elude me, because much of his work is wild. Some favorites of mine are *Nada The Lily, Marie,* and *The Best Short Stories Of Rider Haggard.* If you are like me you will also find yourself, after Haggardizing, dipping back into his contemporaries Kipling and Stevenson, which isn't a bad thing, as Kipling was a terrific storyteller and Stevenson a genius.


CHAPTER SIX
Paul Desmond

The basic record, indeed the basic song, from Paul is the Brubeck Quartet's great *Take Five,* which is still, all these years later, a great record. A basic building block of any decent jazz collection, with Miles Davis's *Kind of Blue,* and work by Johnny Hartman, Chet Baker, Duke Ellington, Billie Holiday, Sarah Vaughn, Marian McPartland, George Gershwin, Johnny Mercer, Cole Porter, Bill Evans, Dexter Gordon, Art Tatum, Count Basie, and the holy man John Coltrane. One of the subtle pleasures of being an American citizen is the sure knowledge that men and women in my country invented jazz. Also basketball, the blues, and gospel music. And Mark Twain and Crazy Horse and Bruce Springsteen and Flannery O'Connor and Abraham Lincoln were born here. For all our immaturity and cruelty this land and its people have created some extraordinary things never before done in the history of the universe.


CHAPTER SEVEN
Jim Kjelgaard

Well, of course you must read the Red trilogy, but then there are any number of Kjelgaard pleasures, and all of them edible in a day or two, which makes them delightful reading for bedside or beach. My own favorites are *Haunt Fox, Swamp Cat, The Black Fawn,* and his very first book, *Forest Patrol,* which is hard to find.

The best of the several websites devoted to Jim and his work is perhaps http://home.sprintmail.com/~charterbus/kjelgaard.htm, which features a sweet essay remembering her dad by his daughter Karen.

Every time I dip back into Kjelgaard (usually prompted by my children, and access to their school library), I end up wandering into other wonderful writers of nature and animals and people, which is a vast thicket of fine writing, among which there are many classics, like Cameron Langford's *The Winter of the Fisher*, and Kenneth Grahame's *The Wind in the Willows*, which is a much more beautifully written book than you remember, and Barry Lopez's *Crow and Weasel*, which is an American classic, and I better stop here or these notes will never end.


CHAPTER EIGHT
Graham Greene


Greene was, according to many modern biographers, a selfish ass of monumental proportions, but he was also a literary artist of surpassing skill and grace and power—such is the mystery of the human character. Readers interested in the story of the man told by himself ought to read his two autobiographies, *A Sort of Life* and *Ways of Escape*. The basic Greene texts, some of which will certainly last as long as people read novels in English, are, I think, *Brighton Rock, The Power and the Glory, The Heart of the Matter, The End of the Affair, The Quiet American, Our Man in Havana*, and *The Human Factor*. If you have never read Greene I'd start with *The Heart of the Matter*, which is even better than the most famous of his novels, *The Power and the Glory*, which is a terrific novel, and arguably one of the great moral texts of all time. *The End of the Affair* was made into an excellent film recently with Ralph Fiennes and Julianne Moore.


CHAPTER NINE
James Joyce


It seems to me, here in my old age, that probably everyone in Western civilization has read about Joyce, and had bits of his work crammed into their syllabi and such, but very few people have really read Joyce for pleasure, and as there is a lot of pleasure and stimulation to be found in James Augustine, I recommend you read or re-read *Dubliners*, which is well-nigh perfect. Then you are on your own.

Me, I love much of *Ulysses*, respect *Portrait of the Artist as a Young Man* (though reading it once was enough), thought *Finnegans Wake* a colossal failure of communication between writer and reader, and detested Joyce's poetry and other prose. *Dubliners,* though—wow.

I note with glee and joy that my clan cousin and very fine Irish writer Roddy Doyle recently (February 2004) caused an uproar in Ireland by saying, bluntly and honestly: "*Ulysses* could have done with a good editor . . . people are always putting *Ulysses* in the top ten books ever written but I doubt that any of those people were really moved by it . . . I only read three pages of *Finnegans Wake* and it was a tragic waste of time . . . *Dubliners* is Joyce's best work."

Sensible man, my man Roddy. Whose novels I recommend without reservation. Start with *The Commitments,* which is also a terrific movie. And this is an interesting discussion that I have with my peculiar friends the McAvoy brothers all the time, about how very rarely a fine novel is made into a fine movie—usually it's the mediocre-to-poor novel that's made into the best movie, and the best books are made into terrible movies, with very rare exceptions like Thomas Berger's *Little Big Man,* and Tolkien's *Lord of the Rings* trilogy, and Joyce Cary's *The Horse's Mouth,* which brings us back to Irish writers, for Cary is one of the very best, and hardly as well known as he should be; so for joyous homework I assign you the entire trilogy of which *The Horse's Mouth* is the closing salvo, the other two books being the slim lovely *Herself Surprised* and *To Be a Pilgrim.*

And further I note happily that another terrific Irish writer, Flann O'Brien, said "I declare to God, if I hear that name Joyce one more time I will surely froth at the gob." Flann makes me laugh. A curious creathur altogether, Mr. O'Brien, whose name wasn't O'Brien, but O'Nolan, although he never used his own name when writing, but wrote journalism as Myles na gCopaleen (in Gaelic, Myles of the Little Horses) and miscellany in the *Irish Times* as Count O'Blather, or James Doe, or Brother Barrabus, or George Knowall. He is best known as the novelist Flann O'Brien, who wrote a classic odd hilarious classic called *At-Swim-Two-Birds,* which if you haven't read it you ought.

CHAPTER TEN
Paul Kelly

The basic Paul record is probably his greatest hits, *Songs from the South,* which gives you lots of flavors of his music, although my personal favorite is his sort-of-bluegrass record, *Smoke,* recorded with the Australian bluegrassy band Uncle Bill. Other essential Pauls for your record collection, if it wishes to boast the Australian Springsteen: *So Much Water So Close To Home, Gossip, Comedy, Hidden Things, Wanted Man, Deeper Water, Live At The Continental and The Esplanade* (a great record), *Words And Music,* and *Nothing But A Dream.*

And while we are on the subject of terrific Australian music, you ought to make a concerted effort to hear as much Archie Roach, Shane Howard, Marcia Howard, and Neil Murray as you can.

SMCL

3 5151 00215 5158